RULE 32 HANDBOOK

POST-CONVICTION RELIEF
PRACTICE MANUAL, CASE LAW
& FORMS

The Essential Guide for:
- Thoroughly Investigating Your Claims
- Utilizing All Options Available to Assess Arguments
- Drafting Comprehensive Legal Arguments
- Writing Compelling Petitions for Post-Conviction Relief
- Maximizing Opportunities to Secure an Evidentiary Hearing
- Presenting Your Claims to the Court of Appeals
- Preserving Your Federal Claims

THE HOPKINS LAW OFFICE
A Professional Corporation

Cedric Martin Hopkins, Esq.
10645 N. Oracle Rd., #121-326
Tucson, Ariz. 85737
(520) 465-2658
objectionyourhonor@hotmail.com

A NOTE ABOUT COPYRIGHT LAW AND THIS MANUAL

TOP COPYRIGHT MYTHS:

- **Everything on the Internet is 'public domain' and free to use.**

  FALSE: Works on the Internet are publicly accessible but are not in the 'public domain' as it pertains to copyright laws. A work is only considered in the 'public domain' (and thereby free to use without any infringement) when the copyright expires.

- **Any work without a copyright notice is not protected.**

  FALSE: Prior to January 1, 1978, this was true. Since that date, copyright protection attaches as soon as the author's idea is put into tangible form.

- **If I change someone else's work I can claim it as my own.**

  FALSE: Simply changing someone else's work is a prohibited act. Any adaptation will be legally regarded as a 'derived work' and will still be considered the original author's work.

- **It's okay to use another person's work if I don't make money from it.**

  FALSE: Unless you have permission to do so, you cannot use another's work regardless if you make money or not from the use of the work. And with respect to this specific handbook, you need written permission from the author to use any portion of the work.

- **I can copy 10% of a work without it constituting infringement.**

  FALSE: Any unauthorized copying, publication or use of a copyrighted work is strictly prohibited and is infringement.

HOW TO USE THIS HANDBOOK

If you're reading this then more than likely you are (1) sitting in a prison you don't want to be in, (2) serving time you don't want to be serving and (3) needing to write a petition for post-conviction relief that you may not know how to write. This handbook was written to assist you with number 3, which will hopefully help you out with 1 and 2.

Several forms have been provided with this handbook. The provided forms are essential in properly preparing a pro per petition for post-conviction relief. The forms will help you organize your petition and offer you a more professional look and feel to the pleadings that you will need to file with the court during the Rule 32 process.

It is often said that a petition for post-conviction relief carries more weight if it is filed by an attorney. That may be somewhat true. Another truth, however, is that a well-written petition (from an attorney or inmate) is highly valued by judges.

In my time clerking for a judge, I reviewed a number of petitions for post-conviction relief, some from attorneys, others from inmates. There was a consensus among all of the law clerks I worked with: we didn't care who wrote the petition, as long as it was well organized and to the point.

Some attorneys know how to organize their pleadings and write in a clear, concise manner while still making a strong, persuasive point. Others don't. The issue for inmates is that their pleadings are far too often unorganized and mix points of law with each other, which often waters down the power of their pleadings. This handbook provides guidance to writing a powerful petition—one that will not only be read and understood by the judge, but will be effective, as well.

Some of the forms provided may be copied and used multiple times. Some of the forms have lines for your writing and others do not. Some forms (like the pro per petition for post-conviction relief) don't have lines for your writing because there would be too many lines on the pages, which would be a distraction for the reader.

HINT: For the forms that do not have lines you should use a piece of paper as a straight edge and lightly pencil in lines, write your petition in ink (black, not blue) using those lines and then go back and erase the pencil lines. This will make your petition (and other pleadings) have a more finished look to them.

ATTORNEY-CLIENT RELATIONSHIP

No attorney-client relationship exists by the purchase of this handbook. This handbook is provided as an explanation of Rule 32.1, et seq. and a roadmap to help you navigate through the post-conviction relief process. This handbook does not, in any way, create an attorney-client relationship with anyone who purchases it or receives it.

The information and tips in this handbook are suggestions only and do not have to be followed blindly. You are free to use your own techniques and pull from this handbook what you feel is beneficial to preparing a successful pro per petition for post-conviction relief. You are in no way bound, compelled or forced to use the suggestions made in this handbook.

In order for you to form an attorney-client relationship with the author of this handbook, a written and signed agreement needs to be in place.

TABLE OF CONTENTS

1. WHAT IS RULE 32?

Arizona Rules of Criminal Procedure, Rule 32.1, *et seq.*, is an Arizona Supreme Court made rule. That means Rule 32 is different from the charges in your indictment that have the "A.R.S." listed after them. The "A.R.S." numbers are statutes, which are made by the Arizona State Legislature. Rule 32, on the other hand, was made by the Arizona Supreme Court to address a specific issue. And on August 1, 1975, the Court brought into existence Rule 32 so that convicted defendants could have a remedy if they pled guilty or if they received ineffective assistance of counsel (and several other reasons we'll get to shortly).

Just as the Arizona Supreme Court brought Rule 32 in existence, they are able to terminate it as well. While them discontinuing the rule is highly unlikely, it is still a possibility.

Rule 32 allows defendants who plead guilty and defendants who went to trial have an opportunity to have their case reviewed for specific violations of their rights under Arizona and/or federal law.

The specific grounds for relief under Rule 32 are as follows:

Rule 32.1 (a): The conviction or the sentence was in violation of the Constitution of the United States or of the State of Arizona.

Rule 32.1(b): The court was without jurisdiction to render the judgment or to impose sentence.

Rule 32.1(c): The sentence imposed exceeded the maximum authorized by law, or is otherwise not in accordance with the sentence authorized by law.

Rule 32.1(d): The person is being held in custody after the sentence imposed has expired.

Rule 32.1(e): Newly discovered materials facts probably exist and such facts probably would have changed the verdict or sentence. Newly discovered materials facts exist if:
1. The newly discovered materials facts were discovered after the trial
2. The defendant exercised due diligence in securing the newly discovered material facts.
3. The newly discovered material facts are not merely cumulative or used solely for impeachment, unless the impeachment evidence substantially undermines testimony which was of critical significance at trial such that the evidence probably would have changed the verdict or sentence.

Rule 32.1(f): The defendant's failure to file a notice of post-conviction relief of-right or notice of appeal within the prescribed time was without fault on the defendant's part.

Rule 32.1(g): There has been a significant change in the law that if determined to apply to defendant's case would probably overturn the defendant's conviction or sentence.

Rule 32.1(h): The defendant demonstrates by clear and convincing evidence that the facts underlying the claim would be sufficient to establish that no reasonable fact-finder would have found defendant guilty of the underlying offense beyond a reasonable doubt, or that the court would not have imposed the death penalty.

The most popular claim alleged by defendants—but is not specifically listed within Rule 32.1—is an ineffective assistance of counsel claim. Ineffective assistance of counsel claims, or IAC claims, make up the vast majority of Rule 32 cases. Rule 32.1(a), is the proper subsection to the Rule to raise IAC claims because a defendant is entitled to effective representation under the United States and Arizona constitutions. If an attorney fails to provide effective representation, for whatever reason or by any circumstance, a defendant may raise that claim under Rule 32.1(a). There will be much more on this claim later.

A. RULE 31 VS. RULE 32

There are several differences between Rule 31 and Rule 32. Rule 31 is the rule that covers your direct appeal if you were unsuccessful following a trial, either to a judge or jury. If you took your case to trial and lost, your trial attorney should have filed a Notice of Appeal on your behalf immediately following sentencing (not after the sentencing minute entry was filed with the clerk, but immediately following the oral pronouncement of your sentence). See, Rule 26.16(a), Ariz.R.Crim.Proc.

The Notice of Appeal has to be filed within 20 days of the date the judge enters judgment and sentences you. If you were sentenced to death, then under Rule 31.2(b) the Clerk of the Court automatically files the Notice of Appeal – your lawyer doesn't have to do anything to start your appeal.

Another significant difference between Rule 31 (Appeal) and Rule 32 (Post-Conviction Relief) is that the Court of Appeals will not consider ineffective assistance of counsel claims under Rule 31. So if you are filing a direct appeal after your lawyer filed an *Anders* brief, then you cannot (or at least, should not) raise any issues regarding how your lawyer did something wrong. Save it for Rule 32. The Court of Appeals will not rule on IAC claims on direct appeal.

B. WHAT RULE 32 IS NOT!

Over the years, I've seen and heard a few myths about what can happen with Rule 32. The most common phrase I hear is, "I want to do my Rule 32 *time reduction*." Rule 32 isn't simply to reduce your prison sentence. And, in fact, it rarely addresses that specific issue.

In order to specifically argue a "time reduction," there would have to be something illegal with your prison sentence. In other words, the judge aggravated your sentence when she wasn't supposed to, or the law that you were sentenced under didn't actually call for as high of a prison sentence as you received. Of course, you can argue that certain mitigation wasn't presented that should have been presented to the judge, but that mitigation has to be extreme, such as you have Hepatitis or a significant brain injury that causes you cognitive delay and your attorney failed to raise this mitigation previously.

The more common way to reduce your prison sentence is to argue that you would have accepted a plea agreement if your lawyer would have properly advised you about the plea or told you about the plea that you didn't know about previously, or told you about specific evidence that you didn't know about when you rejected the plea. In these instances (and there are others we'll get to later), the court may allow you to have the plea agreement extended to you again. See, *State v. Donald*, 198 Ariz. 406.

2. **FILING THE NOTICE OF POST-CONVICTION RELIEF (NOT THE PETITION)**

Rule 32 or Post-Conviction Relief proceedings don't start until your direct appeal has been decided and is completely over with. That means if you had a trial, you should first appeal your convictions and sentences with the Court of Appeals and Arizona Supreme Court (under Rule 31), and then file your Notice of Post-Conviction Relief with the Superior Court (under Rule 32).

If you file your Notice of Post-Conviction Relief before doing your appeal, then you could end up losing your right to appeal, and/or losing the ability to raise some claims that would only be brought up on appeal (like your appellate counsel was ineffective in failing to raise a certain issue). Plus, you might end up having Rule 32 claims that are precluded. (We'll get to preclusion later – it's a nasty, nasty word in Rule 32-land). For those of you who have accepted a plea agreement from the State, you immediately start your Rule 32 proceedings. You won't be filing anything with the Court of Appeals to start your post-conviction proceedings—you file the Notice of Post-Conviction Relief to get your Rule 32 case started. Again, direct appeal proceedings under Rule 31 are only available to those defendants who lost a trial.

A. GETTING YOUR CASE STARTED

After you have completed your direct appeal proceedings, or if you've accepted a plea agreement and have been sentenced, then it's time to file the Notice of Post-Conviction Relief. **(See, Form #1 — *Notice of Post-Conviction Relief*)**

Filling out the Notice of Post-Conviction Relief correctly is critical. Not only do you need to be input the necessary information, the notice gives important information to the judge and attorney who will be assigned to represent you for your Rule 32 proceedings.

The notice indicates who your trial attorney was and who handled your appeal, if you had one. You also have to notate if you are going to be pursuing an ineffective assistance of counsel claim. A section that is often overlooked is the facts of your claim section.

CRITICAL TIP: Filling out the facts supporting your claim is vital because it will be the first impression the judge and assigned attorney get of your case. If you fail to fill it out, then your attorney will not have any idea why you filed the notice. And if you fill it out in a way that is confusing or unclear, then the assigned attorney could also be confused as to what your claims are.

It is important to relate specific facts in a clear manner to give your notice a punch from the very beginning. Also, it is a better practice to keep it short. Less is more.

B. DON'T BE TARDY

Rule 32.4(a) allows you 90 days after the entry of judgment and sentence (that's after you've been sentenced) OR 30 days after the Court of Appeals or Arizona Supreme Court makes a ruling on your appeal to file the Notice of Post-Conviction Relief. The 90-day time limit applies to defendants who plead guilty and have entered into a plea agreement. That is because defendants who plead guilty do not have a right to appeal their convictions and/or sentences under Rule 31 (Direct Appeal). You only can appeal to the Court of Appeals directly by going to trial and losing.

For the defendants who take their case to trial and lose, they appeal the conviction to the Arizona Court of Appeals and then, if they lose the appeal, file a Petition for Review with the Arizona Supreme Court. Once the Arizona Supreme Court issues it's decision, then

Rule 32.4(a) gives you only 30 days (not 90 days) to file the Notice of Post-Conviction Relief.

1. WAIT! I'M LATE!

So you received a letter from your lawyer indicating that the appeal has been denied and he enclosed a copy of the memorandum decision. He failed to inform you that you had to file a Notice of Post-Conviction Relief within 30 days, or he said he would take care of filing the Notice on your behalf. You wait for a few weeks and write to him. No response. You write to the clerk of the court and ask what's going on. They don't tell you much—only that your case was before the Court of Appeals but no Notice of Post-Conviction Relief has been filed. Panic sets in.

You immediately write the judge a letter explaining that you didn't know (weren't advised) of the deadline and what to file, or that your lawyer told you that he was going to file the notice. If the judge is an understanding judge, she would consider your letter to her to be your Notice of Post-Conviction Relief and let the Rule 32 proceedings begin. If not, then you will have to file an untimely Notice of Post-Conviction Relief.

Stop worrying. They have a rule for you. Here it is:

[Rule 32.1(f): "The defendant's failure to file a notice of post-conviction relief of-right or notice of appeal within the prescribed time was without fault on the defendant's part."]

File your Notice of Post-Conviction Relief and cite (which means to write out) **Rule 32.1(f)**, and explain your situation as to why you are filing a late notice. The judge will most likely appoint a lawyer for you and start the Rule 32 proceedings as if your notice was timely.

2. THE CORRECT COURT

So you have the Notice of Post-Conviction Relief in your hands and can't wait to get your post-conviction proceedings started. But where do you send it? You send the Notice of Post-Conviction Relief to the same Superior Court where you were sentenced. So if you were sentenced in Pima County Superior Court, you send it to the Clerk of the Court at the Pima County Superior Court, and if you were sentenced in the Maricopa County Superior Court, then you send it to that court.

Here are the addresses to the Superior Courts in Arizona:

Apache County Superior Court
P.O. Box 667
70 West 3rd South
St. Johns, Ariz. 85936
Ph: 928-337-7555
Fax: 928-337-7586

Cochise County Superior Court
Sierra Vista
100 Colonia de Salud
Sierra Vista, Ariz. 85635
Ph: 520-803-3060
Fax: 520-458-4148

Cochise County Superior Court
Bisbee
100 Quality Hill
P.O. Box CK
Bisbee, Ariz. 85603
Ph: 520-432-8570
Fax: 520-432-4850

Coconino County Superior Court
200 N. San Francisco St.
Flagstaff, Ariz. 86001
Ph: 928-679-7600

Gila County Superior Court
1400 E. Ash St.
Globe, Ariz. 85501
Ph: 928-425-3231
1-800-304-4452 (In-State only)

Graham County Superior Court
800 W. Main St., 2nd Floor
Safford, Ariz. 85546
Ph: 928-428-3100

Greenlee County Superior Court
223 Fifth St.
P.O. Box 1027
Clifton, Ariz. 85533
Ph: 928-865-4242
Fax: 928-865-5358

La Paz County Superior Court
1316 Kofa Ave., Suite 607
Parker, Ariz. 85344
Ph: 928-669-6131
Fax: 928-669-2186

Maricopa County Superior Court
201 W. Jefferson
Phoenix, Ariz. 85003
Ph: 602-506-3204
Alt. Ph: 602-506-8575

Mohave County Superior Court
401 E. Spring Street
P.O. Box 7000
Kingman, Ariz. 86402
Ph: 928-753-0713

Navajo County Superior Court
P.O. Box 668
Holbrook, Ariz. 86025
Ph: 928-524-4171
Alt. Ph: 928-524-4185

Pima County Superior Court
110 W. Congress
Tucson, Ariz. 85701
Ph: 520-724-3200
Fax: 520-798-3531

Pinal County Superior Court
971 Jason Lopez Circle, Building A
Florence, Ariz. 85132
Ph: 520-866-5400
Fax: 520-866-5401

Santa Cruz Superior Court
2160 N. Congress Dr.
Nogales, Ariz. 85621
Ph: 520-375-7700

Yavapai County Superior Court
120 South Cortez Street
Prescott, Ariz. 86303
Ph: 928-771-3312
Fax: 928-771-3111

Yuma County Superior Court
2440 West 28th Street
Yuma, Ariz. 85364
Ph: 928-817-4083
Fax: 928-817-4091

3. YOU'VE SUCCESSFULLY FILED THE NOTICE...SO, WHAT HAPPENS NEXT?

After you file the Notice of Post-Conviction Relief with the correct court, then you should receive a notice back from the court that will give you helpful information.

The notice will let you know that the case is proceeding forward, that you are in the correct court and, most importantly, indicate the lawyer who will be representing you. Most counties will provide a deadline for the court reporters to prepare the transcripts and a deadline for your previous attorneys to make your files available or transferred to your new Rule 32 lawyer.

Keep track of all deadlines—you'll need to notify the court of missed deadlines by court reporters, attorneys or any other individual who misses a deadline.

If you took your case to trial, lost the trial and had an appeal, chances are your appellate attorney has already sent to you a copy of your trial transcripts and record on appeal. Don't worry. You won't have to send those documents to your new Rule 32 attorney. The Rule 32 attorney will be responsible for getting those documents (record on appeal, transcripts and trial file) from a source other than you.

Having said that, there have been extremely rare instances where a judge has ordered that a defendant send the transcripts to the Rule 32 attorney. With most counties having electronic versions of the transcripts available to Rule 32 counsel, this issue is not likely to surface. But if somehow you have the original trial file, you will most likely have to send it to your Rule 32 attorney.

CRITICAL TIP: If you have to send the trial file (or any other large mailing) to your attorney, ask the attorney to get pre-approval of the cost of mailing (usually around $20.00 for a bankers box) from either the Office of Public Defense Services (Maricopa County) or the Office of Court-Appointed Counsel (Pima County) or the court administrator for all other counties. Once the attorney has pre-approval for the expense of mailing the large file, the attorney can pay to have you mail the file—that way, you won't spend money from your prison account to mail the file.

C. WORKING WITH YOUR COURT-APPOINTED COUNSEL

The Court will either appoint a lawyer from a public agency (Public Defender's Office, Legal Advocate's Office, Legal Defender's Office, etc.) or a private attorney who is on the county's panel to accept Rule 32 cases. The difference between a Public Defender, Legal Advocate or a Legal Defender and a private appointed attorney is that the private attorney works for himself or herself whereas the attorney who works for an agency (Public Defender, Legal Advocate or Legal Defender) does not. The private appointed attorneys are on panels for various counties in Arizona and have agreed to accept appeals and/or post-conviction relief cases on a reduced fee basis.

1. COMMUNICATION MATTERS (HOW TO COMMUNICATE WITH YOUR COURT-APPOINTED LAWYER)

The goal of having a court-appointed lawyer is to get that lawyer invested into your case. More likely than not, your court-appointed lawyer has a large number of appointed cases, and if you have an appointed lawyer, they also have other retained cases. Therefore, you need to get their attention, and get them working actively on your case.

The most common form of communication you'll have with your attorney is going to be by letter via the U.S. Mail. The key to writing an effective letter to your lawyer is to be brief. A 12-page letter is less likely to get read thoroughly than a 1-3 page letter. And the key to getting 12 pages worth of information into one or two pages is: get to the point.

If you feel that your trial attorney did not advise you properly, state exactly what your attorney did wrong, preferably in bullet-point style. Writing page after page about how your attorney showed up late to hearings repeatedly, or was dressed inappropriately is going to get your letter skimmed over instead of being fully considered by your attorney.

CRITICAL TIP: The letters to your court-appointed lawyer should be short and to the point. While your family, children, etc. are important to you and that's why you need to get out of prison, or whatever other reason you give for needing to get out of prison, those reasons are irrelevant to your Rule

32 attorney. **The attorney only needs to know about legal reason why your case should be dismissed, why you should be resentenced or you should be given a new trial or withdrawn from the plea agreement. Anything else is unnecessary fluff that is likely to get skimmed over and water down your stronger points. Everyone has a compelling reason they want to get out of prison, not everyone has a strong legal issue to raise— make sure to highlight your strong legal issue, not family issues.**

2. **OBLIGATIONS OF A COURT-APPOINTED LAWYER**

With respect to documents, your attorney is required to get a copy of your trial file, transcripts and the court record. Your attorney is also obligated to contact you via letter or phone call to keep you advised of the status of the case. Those are the basic obligations that your Rule 32 attorney has after being appointed and prior to the petition being filed.

Once your attorney has all of the documents necessary to properly review your case, then the investigation aspect of your case begins. Usually, the client (you) will provide the attorney with different issues to investigate. For example, your trial attorney may not have called a witness at trial that you feel would have been helpful to your case. Your Rule 32 attorney should track that witness down and interview him or her. In one case, it took over one year, two investigators and a few court orders to track down a witness. Another example may be a document that you feel your attorney should have gotten, but didn't, such as a receipt, auto policy or lease—all of which have proven to be valuable documents in cases.

At the risk of stating the obvious, your attorney is obligated to review the case and file either a petition for post-conviction relief raising any issues that he or she feels are legitimate issues under Rule 32, or files a Notice of Completion (in Maricopa County) or Notice in Lieu of Petition for Post-Conviction Relief (in Pima County). Because you're reading this, your attorney most likely filed one of the notices, which tells the court that he or she did not feel that there were any issues to raise under Rule 32.

Once your attorney files a notice informing the court that he or she feels there are no issues to raise under Rule 32, the court is obligated to allow you file a pro per petition for post-conviction relief and will set a due date for your pro per petition. You are free to raise any issues you feel are justified under Rule 32 in your pro per petition.

3. **WHAT YOUR COURT-APPOINTED LAWYER IS NOT OBLIGATED TO DO**

Communicating With Your Family Members

One common issue that comes up in Rule 32 cases is that clients want their attorney to update their family members as to the status of the Rule 32 case. The attorney is only obligated to do so if communicating with your family member relates to a potential issue in the petition for post-conviction relief. Otherwise, any communicating the attorney does with the family member is simply the attorney being gracious. Rule 32 attorneys are not obligated to communicate with your family members.

Sending You Case Law

The State Bar of Arizona has made it clear that attorneys do not need to print cases and send them to pro se clients. Some attorneys, however, do provide case law and other legal materials to clients. So if you send a letter requesting case law, make sure that you ask nicely, don't demand. If you demand that your attorney send you case law, or any thing *other than* the trial file, transcripts and/or court records, you probably won't receive them.

Sending You Other Materials

Over the years, I have received a request for just about everything you can think of: paper, pens, pencils, legal pads, stamps, money, food, law books, practice guides, expando folders...everything. Your Rule 32 attorney does not need to provide any of these materials to you. The only items that he or she needs to provide are the record, transcripts and trial file.

4. WILL YOU CERTIFY?

Rule 32.5 requires that the defendant make a declaration that the issues contained within the petition for post-conviction relief (prepared by an attorney) are the only issues known to the defendant and the only issues that will be raised in the petition for post-conviction relief.

Here's the portion of Rule 32.5 regarding certification: "The petition shall be accompanied by a declaration by the defendant stating under penalty of perjury that the information contained is true to the best of the defendant's knowledge and belief." Rule 32.5.

The attorney who prepares your petition for post-conviction relief will need to include that declaration. If you file your petition without that declaration the judge will strike your petition and give you 30 days to file the petition again with the declaration.

D. GOING PRO PER

This section and the sections going forward are the main motivation for preparing this Rule 32 Manual. Up until this point in the Manual, an attorney was representing you in your Rule 32 case. Once your attorney files a Notice of Completion or Notice in Lieu of a Petition for Post-Conviction Relief indicating to the court that no issues will be raised in a petition for post-conviction relief, the case shifts to you. You will now be responsible for filing a timely pro per petition for post-conviction relief and raising the issues that you want the judge to decide in your case.

1. PRO PER V. PRO SE

You may hear, read or see the terms pro per and/or pro se. Lawyers and judges use the terms interchangeably. For purposes of filing your petition for post-conviction relief, the two terms mean the same thing: you are representing yourself. Technically, the two terms refer to a certain form of jurisdiction, but in your case, the court already has jurisdiction over you so it is irrelevant which term you use.

2. How Do You Know You're Pro Per?

The first indication that you are going to be representing yourself will be the Notice of Completion or Notice in Lieu of the Petition for Post-Conviction Relief that is filed and mailed to you by your Rule 32 attorney. As explained above, that notice gives notice to the judge and prosecutor that the lawyer who filed the notice did not find any viable claims (in his or her opinion) to raise under Rule 32.

The next document you should receive (other than a letter from your lawyer explaining the pro per process and what to expect next) is a notice or order from the court. The court's notice/order will direct your Rule 32 lawyer to send you materials, order that you are now representing yourself and set a due date for your petition to be filed. The other due date that the judge will set is a date by which your Rule 32 attorney is to mail you your file.

Pay close attention to that date. If the due date for your Rule 32 attorney to mail the file to you passes and you still have not received your file, then you need to write a letter to your Rule 32 attorney requesting the file. If you do not get a response from your Rule 32 attorney within two weeks, then you need to write to the clerk of the court and/or judge handling your case and inform them that you have not received the file. Make sure to create a written record (letters and filings with the court) of your requests to obtain the file. And then once you receive the file, go through it thoroughly and note any documents/items that are missing, such as plea agreements, transcripts, etc.

If you have missing documents/items, then you need to make another written request for the specific items. Again, keep a written record of your requests for the additional documents/items.

3. Avoiding Legal Beagles

In every prison, in every city and in every state there are "legal beagles." Legal beagles are inmates who have learned an area of the law and want to offer you advice about your case. In just about every situation, they are looking to get something from you in exchange for their advice. And in just about every situation, their advice is not worth whatever it was you gave to them for that advice. The legal beagles will tell you that you have a solid case even if you don't just so you will pay them to write a petition. Be leery of these legal beagles and what they are selling.

E. Obtaining The Record, Transcripts And Trial File

As I explained in Section D(2), your Rule 32 lawyer is responsible for sending the file to you. Exactly what makes up "the file" varies with each attorney and each case. At a minimum, you need to obtain copies (or originals) of the transcripts in your case, the file the trial attorney used (even if you accepted a plea agreement it's called "the trial file") and the documents that were filed with the court. If you had an appeal, the documents that were filed with the clerk of the court are collected and put into what's called a Record on Appeal. If you accepted a plea agreement, you'll have to collect your own record, which should consist of the documents filed by the prosecutor and your lawyer with the clerk of the court. The attorney who was assigned to represent you with respect to your Rule 32 should send you those records.

1. **YOUR RIGHT TO PREPARE**

The judge who reviews your pro per petition for post-conviction relief (pro per petition) will hold you to a high standard, as will the Court of Appeals and all other courts who review your case afterwards. As a part of that standard, you will be expected to file with your pro per petition any and all documents that support your petition. If you fail to do so, then in all likelihood, you won't be permitted to bring those documents before the judge at any future time.

The nature of Rule 32 is that you have one chance to argue ALL of your issues. There are very specific and very rare instances where you can bring a second (or what is called, successive) Rule 32 petition.

Because you are going to be held to a high standard when filing your pro per petition, you have the right to review the necessary documents to support your petition. When requesting documents from the lawyer who handled your Rule 32 case, make sure to be specific as to which documents you need and why you need them. Do not simply list a large number of documents and demand them. I have known attorneys who have received those lists and filed a notice with the court asking which documents are to be supplied to the defendant. There is a good chance the judge will order that you only get a limited number of the documents you requested.

CRITICAL TIP: The better practice is to be respectful and pleasant with your Rule 32 lawyer when asking for documents. It would also be wise to break up your requests for any large list of documents. Having said that, if you are requesting either the transcripts and/or the record on appeal, you have the right to those documents, so you can be more demanding. Just remember, you may have to ask this same lawyer for a favor later on. If you've been rude or demanding to him or her, chances are you won't get the favor granted.

If you are not having good communication with your attorney via letters, then ask your counselor (COIII) to set up a legal call with your attorney so you can speak to him or her over the phone. Sometimes talking with the attorney can help smooth things over if communication has been shaky. In addition, often what one person writes is misinterpreted by the person reading the letter. Speaking to one another will clarify things.

2. **TRIAL ATTORNEY, APPELLATE ATTORNEY, RULE 32 ATTORNEY—WHO IS SUPPOSED TO SEND YOU WHAT, EXACTLY**

Let's break it down a little further as to who is supposed to send you what materials:

Trial Attorney
Again, this person is the lawyer you went to trial with and/or accepted a plea agreement with. The trial attorney should not have to send you any documents. The reason for that is because your Rule 32 attorney should have requested and received the trial file from the trial attorney. The only way the trial attorney should have the trial file is if the Rule 32 attorney sent the trial file back to the trial attorney, which would be odd because your Rule 32 attorney should know that he or she is required to pass along that file to you.

If you receive the trial file (from either the trial attorney or Rule 32 attorney) and there are documents missing or other documents from the file you need, then you should request those documents first from the trial attorney. Get that person to say that they do not have the requested document and then request it from your Rule 32 attorney. If the document is not with the trial attorney, then it should be with the Rule 32 attorney.

Rule 32 Attorney
The majority of your materials will come from your Rule 32 attorney. The Rule 32 attorney is responsible for collecting the materials that are needed to properly review your case. Typically, those materials include the trial file (with police reports, attorney notes (those are not confidential if you're alleging ineffective assistance of counsel), all disclosure from the State, pleadings that were filed and correspondence (letters and emails) regarding your case), the appellate record (if you had a trial) and the transcripts.

The Rule 32 attorney will only (or should only) send the materials to you once the trial court orders him or her to do so. That order is issued after your Rule 32 attorney files a notice indicating that there is no issue that will be raised by that attorney and the judge accepts that notice and orders that you proceed pro per. In that same order, the judge will typically set a deadline for the Rule 32 attorney to send you all materials in his or her possession.

Be sure to contact the attorney if you have not received the materials by the due date. And if you do not get a response from the attorney within ten (10) days, then write a letter to the judge indicating that you have not received the materials. It is important to keep a written record of your activities on the case so that if it becomes an issue later you won't have to rely upon your memory. In addition, issues often arise where it will be your word against another person's word—make sure your word is written down (and preferably filed with the court).

Appellate Attorney
If you had a trial, then you more than likely had an appeal. If the attorney who represented you during your sentencing hearing did not file a notice of appeal and you did not have a direct appeal under Rule 31 (which would have been before the Court of Appeals and not the Superior Court), then you should request a delayed appeal under **Rule 32.1(f)**.

If your appeal is finished, then your appellate attorney should have sent to you the record on appeal and the transcripts of the trial and sentencing. Even though your appellate attorney has sent the transcripts and record on appeal to you, you may receive a second copy from your Rule 32 attorney. Again, the record on appeal consists of all pleadings that were filed in your case, minute entries, the jury instructions, and any exhibits that were admitted at trial.

Between your trial attorney, Rule 32 attorney and your appellate attorney, you should receive all of the materials you need to properly prepare your pro per petition for post-conviction relief. What if you need more documents? Go to Section F.

F.   How To Get Other Documents, Exhibits And Witnesses

Often times, even after receiving all of the materials from your attorneys you will need more documents, videos, records and/or statements from people. There are three main avenues to explore in order to obtain those materials.

1.   Subpoena Power – Yes, You Have It!

A subpoena is a court order that directs a person to appear at a certain place, at a certain time and on a certain date. A subpoena can also be a court order that directs a person or company to make documents, records or videos available to you. While preparing your pro per petition for post-conviction relief, you can use the subpoena power of the court. **(See, Form #2—*Subpoena Form*)**

A Proper Way To Use Your Subpoena Power
Prior to issuing a subpoena for someone or a company, the better practice is to write them a letter and request in writing the materials you need. Be sure to explain why you need the materials and give as much information as possible to allow them to make an informed decision. Most likely, you will get the materials from your written request.

If you do not receive the materials from your written request, then you should follow up with a subpoena. By filling out, copying and filing a subpoena with the Superior Court that you were sentenced in, you will receive the subpoena back from the court. It will be your responsibility to serve the subpoena on the person/company that you are requesting materials from. To do that, you can mail the subpoena along with an acceptance of service form. **(See, Form #3—*Acceptance of Service Form*)**

The person receiving the subpoena and the acceptance of service form can sign the form and return it to you, which will show that the subpoena was properly served. You then file the acceptance of service form with the clerk of the court.

Another option to serve the subpoena is to write to your Advisory Counsel (Your Rule 32 attorney becomes your Advisory Counsel once you are acting pro per) and ask them to serve the subpoena for you.

2.   Court Request

If you are seeking to compel disclosure from the prosecutor (or any other party who does not comply with the subpoenas), then you will need the court's assistance to do so. Compelling disclosure in Rule 32 cases can prove to be difficult, if not improbable.

Under *Canion v. Cole*, 210 Ariz. 598 (2005), the Arizona Supreme Court made it so that a defendant has to file the notice *and petition for post-conviction relief* showing a valid claim before the trial court can compel disclosure. In terms of properly preparing a petition for post-conviction relief, this ruling puts the cart before the horse. In other words, the Arizona Supreme Court in *Canion* makes you file your petition prior to you receiving the compelling disclosure that would support your petition in the first place. Only after you file your petition showing that you have valid claims will the court compel disclosure.

(See, Form #4—*Motion to Compel Discovery*)

A motion to compel is the last option that should be used to obtain the materials you are seeking. The *Canion* court decision made clear that any court-ordered discovery requests is at the pure discretion of the court and only AFTER you have filed the petition for post-conviction relief "to provide context for the motion to compel." In nearly every instance, you will want the material prior to filing your pro per petition for post-conviction relief.

3. INVESTIGATORS

While you may not be able to compel disclosure by court order prior to filing your petition, you can request to have an investigator assigned to your case to help you find potential witnesses, help serve subpoenas and other specific investigative tasks. Some counties actually have a detailed list of the tasks they will pay an investigator to perform—anything not on the list doesn't get paid.

The most effective way to get an investigator assigned to your case is by contacting your Advisory Counsel. Write to your Advisory Counsel and let them know you want an investigator. Request a specific number of hours that you will need the investigator, such as 10 hours. More time can be added later.

There is a process for assigning an investigator to your case in each county. Each county has a panel of investigators and once a request is made, one of the investigators is assigned to your case. Your Advisory Counsel will need to get approval (not from the court) for the investigator but it is not difficult to do.

CRITICAL TIP: After an investigator is assigned to your case, be sure to get that person's contact information and communicate with them directly, not through your Advisory Counsel. You should keep your Advisory Counsel up-to-date as to the status of your investigation, but once you have an investigator, that person is the most important person to collect the documents, find the people, etc. that you need to properly prepare your petition for post-conviction relief.

INTERPRETERS: The process for obtaining an investigator is the same for getting an interpreter on your case. In some cases, it is necessary for you to have a letter or other document interpreted in order to prepare your petition for post-conviction relief. Again, request that an interpreter be assigned to your case through your Advisory Counsel. And if you write to your lawyer in Spanish, your lawyer can have that letter interpreted. Just know that communication with your lawyer will be somewhat delayed because the letter has to be sent to the interpreter and then sent back to the attorney.

Attorneys are able to write back in Spanish using interpreting software that can be found on the Internet. They should send an English and Spanish version of the letter. Often times, inmates are being assisted by other inmates and those other inmates may not read/speak Spanish.

G. COMMUNICATING WITH THE COURT AND PROSECUTOR

Prior to going pro per, you probably did not have much contact with the court or prosecutor. Now that you are acting pro per, you are required to communicate with both the court (meaning the judge and the clerk of court) and the prosecutor. In doing so, always maintain a high level of respect and be courteous.

1. FILING NOTICES AND MOTIONS

The first notice that you filed with respect to Rule 32 is the Notice of Post-Conviction Relief (**Form #1**). That form started the Rule 32 proceedings. Now that you are acting pro per, you will be required to file other notices, motions and requests with the court.

A motion is a document you draft (write) that asks the Court for something. (See, Form #4 – Motion to Compel for an example). The caption of a motion is the box that has "State of Arizona v. [Defendant's Name]" in it. On the other side of the caption is the title of the document, such as "Motion to Extend Time to File Petition for Post-Conviction Relief." The case number and judge's name also goes on the right side of the document, in the same area as the title.

Again, when you file a motion (as compared to a notice), you are asking the Court to do something. It could be anything that you need done on your case, from extending the time to file your petition to changing Advisory Counsel.

Underneath the caption and title is where you write out what you want from the Court. Be clear and concise (brief, not long). It's not how long you talk, but what you put in it that matters. Make sure to ask for certain things, and be specific. Explain the reason you are making the request and any basis you have for the request. Again, be clear and concise.

A notice (as opposed to a motion) is simply letting the court and prosecutor know something happened. You will receive a Notice of Completion or Notice in Lieu of Petition for Post-Conviction Relief if you are acting pro per. Those notices are filed by your attorney and let the court and prosecutor know that they did not find any issue to raise on your behalf.

Other notices you will receive include notices that a file has been transferred to you or another attorney and/or a notice that the state will not be filing a response unless ordered to do so. There can be any number of notices filed with the court and they all are doing the same thing: letting all the parties and judge know that something happened.

When you file a notice or motion, make sure to send a copy to the prosecutor. The prosecutor will always have the opportunity to respond to any document you file. The way they respond is by first receiving a copy of what you filed.

You will know which prosecutor's office to send the motions and notices to because the contact information will be on the pleadings the prosecutor filed in the materials you receive.

i. Timeliness

Whatever you file something with the court make sure to do so in a timely manner. Often, the judge will give you a date by which to file a notice or motion. Be sure to calendar that date and mail out the necessary document on or before that date. As long as the requested document is post-marked by the due date, your document will be considered timely.

ii. Untimely Filings

In the event you mail something out untimely (beyond the due date), then make sure to include a "Motion to Consider [Insert Name Of Motion] Timely Filed." In the Motion to Consider [Name of Motion] Timely Filed explain why the filing is late and that there would be no prejudice to the State for the late filing. Be as specific as you can regarding the reasons for the late filing so the judge can make an informed decision about your late filing. These types of motions are routinely granted.

H. DRAFTING THE PETITION FOR POST-CONVICTION RELIEF

Drafting the pro per petition for post-conviction relief is going to be one of the most difficult parts of your case. Everything up until now has been preparing you to write the petition. Writing an effective petition for post-conviction relief is your only opportunity to convince a judge and/or prosecutor to grant you the relief that you request. You will have to not only ensure that each and every claim is included in the petition, you have to make sure to draft your petition in a way that will preserve your claims for the Court of Appeals and Arizona Supreme Court.

And if you plan on going to federal court with your claims, you will also have to draft your petition in a way that will guard against federal procedural defaults that will keep you out of District Court, the United States Court of Appeals for the Ninth Circuit and the United States Supreme Court. The sections below will instruct you how to properly prepare your petition to preserve all of your claims, rights and opportunities for further review, if necessary.

1. OUTLINE, ORGANIZE, THEN ORGANIZE AGAIN

Organization is the key to success. Write that down and put it up on your wall. Remember it. That's how you will succeed in this and every other project you take on.

With respect to writing your petition for post-conviction relief, the first part of that organization will be to draft an outline of what your petition will look like.

When you have an outline of your petition, it will be much easier to write the petition. You will be able to see (literally) where your petition is headed and which sections you need to focus on. You can also adjust arguments based on how your outline flows and make sure to keep the petition nicely structured. Most importantly, your arguments will be clear and well thought out when you create an outline.

Once you feel like you have created a solid outline, spend a day or two away from the outline, not thinking about it. Afterwards, come back to it and re-read it and see if the arguments still flow nicely and make sense in the order you created them. If so, you have a final outline to work off of.

2. CAPTION PAGE

The caption page is simply the first page of your petition for post-conviction relief or any other pleading you file with the court. A pleading is simply a legal document, usually consisting of the numbers 1-28 along the left-hand side of the page. You don't have to have pleading paper to file the petition (I have provided you with 10 pages of blank pleading paper if you want to use it.)

The caption page will have your contact information in the top-left hand corner of the page. Underneath your contact information, centered in the middle of the page, you will write which court you are filing the pleading in. Underneath the court name, you will write "State of Arizona v. [Your Name] on the left-hand side of the page. Directly opposite of the "State of Arizona" language you need to have three items written down: 1) your case number(s), 2) the name of the document (Motion to...), and 3) the judge's name you are filing the document with. That will complete the caption part of the pleading. Anything written after that is the body of the pleading/petition.

3. INTRODUCTION

The first part of the petition (or any motion) is the introduction paragraph. In that paragraph, you will want to tell the judge your name and then, in just a few sentences, explain which issues you are raising. See the sample petition **(Form #5—*Sample Petition for Post-Conviction Relief*)** for a typical introduction paragraph to your petition.

4. STATEMENT OF FACTS

"Facts are stubborn things." –John Adams, representing English soldiers following the Boston Massacre.

The statement of facts is extremely important to drafting a successful petition for post-conviction. The arguments you make throughout your brief will hinge on the facts that you put into the statement of facts.

One of the first parts of the petition many judges flip to is the statement of facts. In order to have an effective statement of facts, you have to be objective with the facts. That means admitting or conceding certain aspects of your case and focusing on the strong points of your case. Judges, and their law clerks (who often read the petitions prior to the judge even reading them), appreciate it when the statement of facts is objective and not used as an argument—you can do that later in the petition.

CRITICAL TIP: You don't want to leave out a fact or facts just because they are not in your favor. If you do this, and the State puts the damaging facts in their brief, then you will lose credibility. Often times, if you leave out damaging facts, the State will not only mention the damaging facts, but will do everything it can to highlight those facts and the fact that you didn't mention them.

i. *Citing to the Record*

While writing your statement of facts, you should cite to the record. What that means is to tell the judge and prosecutor where you are getting your information.

For Rule 31 direct appeals, the clerk of the court prepares what is called a Record on Appeal. The Record on Appeal, or ROA as it is referred to in briefs, contains all of the court filings by all parties in the case. If you accepted a plea agreement, then you will not have a record on appeal prepared by the clerk. The record you will have (if you pled guilty) will consist of the documents that are gathered by your Rule 32 attorney.

If you went to trial and had a direct appeal and are now in your Rule 32 proceedings, then you will have a record on appeal. Sometimes, Rule 32 attorneys will send you an electronic version of the record on appeal on a CD.

CRITICAL TIP: It is extremely difficult and takes a long time for the prison to allow you to view the contents of a CD, and it often takes a court order. You can prepare a motion to have the electronic records printed out so that you have a hard copy of the record on appeal. The time the prison gives you to view the documents on the CD may not be enough to properly prepare a petition. In addition, you may want to include some of the documents as attachments to your petition.

With petitions for post-conviction relief, you can make your own record. The record you make will mostly be comprised of documents. Documents such as the indictment, plea agreement, and certain minute entries. Those are the basic documents.

You'll also have documents that are specific to your issues and case. For example, if your attorney failed to include a car rental lease to show that you had the right to possess the car and that it was not stolen, then that would be included as part of your record. There are countless other documents that could be a part of your record.

CRITICAL TIP: Do NOT include your presentence report in your record because if it is attached to your petition for post-conviction relief, then it will be made public to everyone. You can refer to the presentence report in your petition if you need to—the judge and prosecutor already have access to it.

The way to include your record in your petition is to attach it to the petition itself. As long as the record isn't too lengthy (no more than 30 or so pages), you can staple both the record and the petition together. If the record is longer than 30 pages, then you should create a separate cover/caption page for the record and file it separately from the petition. The pleading will be labeled "Appendix to Pro Per Petition for Post-Conviction Relief."

When you create your record, separate each full document with pages marked, "Attachment A," "Attachment B," etc. So if you have 10 documents that you are attaching to your petition as your record, then you will want to start the first document off with a page in front of it marked, "Attachment A." After "Attachment A" you should put a short description of the document. So it would read, "Attachment A – Car Rental Lease from Alamo, dated 06/07/13"

And then throughout your petition, when you refer to the car rental lease you will end the sentence citing to Attachment A. So a sentence in your petition would read: "My attorney failed to present the jury with the car rental lease I had given him. See, Attachment A." And every time you mention the lease agreement, you will cite to Attachment A.

Organize the documents that will make up your record prior to writing your petition so that you can easily cite to them while you are writing your petition. Or, you can write your petition and leave the letter of the attachment blank and fill it in later, such as "Attachment ___"

ii. Relevant Facts

Often times defendants want to write out each and every fact that occurred during their case. The statement of facts becomes incredibly long and you lose the reader. The better practice is to only write the facts that are relevant to your argument.

For example, if you are raising an issue about your sentencing and how the judge sentenced you under the incorrect statute, the facts of the crime are irrelevant. What the judge is going to need to know is the crime you were found guilty of (including the statute) and the statute you were sentenced under. The specific details of the crime would be irrelevant, for the most part, in that analysis. Therefore, they aren't needed in the petition.

It's difficult for most attorneys and pro se litigants to only include the relevant facts. Most of the time, people want to reargue their case through the statement of facts. Resist the temptation to reargue your case—you'll have a chance to argue your case later in the petition.

iii. Concise Facts

Now that you know to only include the relevant facts, the second trick is to keep it concise (that means short). Get to the point. More than likely, the people you are arguing your case to already know the facts of the case so it's not necessary to ramble on in the statement of facts. And if you're sticking only to the relevant facts, chances are your statement of facts will be concise.

5. STATEMENT OF FACTS WITHIN YOUR KNOWLEDGE

There are two statements of facts. The first is about the case in general. The second—the statement of facts within your knowledge—consists of what you know specifically about the claims you are making in your petition.

These facts will make up your affidavit. They will be what the judge should consider as true, under Rule 32.

For example, if you were raising a claim of ineffective assistance of counsel, you would state in this Statement of Facts Within Your Knowledge the specific facts behind that claim. That would cover how many times you met with the attorney, or if you saw certain disclosure, etc. These are facts that don't necessarily go in the general statement of facts regarding your case but are needed by the court to decide your case.

Think of it this way: the general statement of facts are facts everyone knows and are part of the record, while the Statement of Facts Within Your Knowledge are facts only you know and are relevant to your claim(s).

6. IDENTIFYING AND LISTING ISSUES

At the beginning of your petition, you'll want to let the court know which issues you will be raising in your petition. The issues will be listed on the front page of the petition or in an introduction paragraph at the beginning of the petition. This isn't a full argument of your issues, only a one-line sentence identifying your issues.

7. PRECLUSION

Now that you have identified the issues you want to raise, you have to make sure that the law allows you to raise them. Rule 32.2 is the preclusion rule. Here's the text of that rule:

"A defendant shall be precluded from relief under this rule based upon any ground: (1) Raisable on direct appeal under Rule 31 or on post-trial motion under Rule 24; (2) Finally adjudicated on the merits on appeal or in any previous collateral proceeding; (3) That has been waived at trial, on appeal, or in any previous collateral proceeding."

The first section of the preclusion rule means that if you went to trial, any issue that you could have raised on appeal is not permitted to be argued in your Rule 32 petition. In other words, you only get one bite at the apple. The key aspect of this section of the preclusion rule is that you can't raise an issue that you *could have raised* on appeal, whether you did or not.

CRITICAL TIP: The most effective way to circumvent the "raised or could have raised" preclusion rule is to argue an ineffective assistance of counsel claim regarding the same issues. For example, you can't re-argue an issue relating to an illegal search warrant directly, but you can argue that the trial attorney didn't effectively challenge an illegal search warrant. When you do this type of argument, you are making two arguments: (1) the ineffective assistance of counsel claim regarding the attorney, and (2) the issue relating to the search warrant and how it was illegal.

It's important to clearly state in your petition that you are not re-arguing the issue of the search warrant but rather a claim of ineffective assistance of counsel. But in order to fully understand and rule on the ineffective assistance of counsel claim, the court will need to know the specific facts regarding the search warrant and if it was a legitimate issue. This ineffective assistance of counsel claim can be raised against the trial attorney and/or the appellate attorney for not raising a legitimate appellate issue.

The "post-trial motion under Rule 24" preclusion aspect of the rule means that if the trial attorney files a Rule 24 motion following the trial, whatever issue that was raised in that motion cannot be raised in your Rule 32 petition for post-conviction relief. Any issue that was brought in a Rule 24 motion in the trial court will most likely be argued with the Court of Appeals anyway. Again, you may be able to "re-argue" the issue under a claim of ineffective assistance of counsel claim described above.

The second section of the preclusion rule ("finally adjudicated on the merits on appeal or in any previous collateral proceeding") means that you are not permitted to raise in your Rule 32 petition any issue that was decided by the

Court of Appeals or the trial court following conviction and sentencing. It's similar to section (a)(1) of the preclusion rule except that (a)(2) deals with claims that were actually made on appeal or in a previous Rule 32, or any other collateral proceeding before the trial court following conviction.

Section (a)(3) of the preclusion rule is similar to (a)(2) in the sense that if you could have raised an issue under Rule 32 in a previous Rule 32 proceeding, then it will be precluded. The other aspect of this rule is that the trial attorney may waive an issue under Rule 32, but if that is the case, then it would form the basis for an ineffective assistance of counsel.

Preclusion has to be raised by the State (See, Rule 32.2(c)), you don't have to explain how your grounds are not precluded—that's the State's job. And if they don't allege it in their response to your petition for post-conviction relief, then it should be considered waived. I say "should be" because the rule says "any court on review" can find that your issue(s) is precluded. The specific rule states "...any court on review of the record may determine and hold that an issue is precluded regardless of whether the state raises preclusion."

8. **RELEVANT AND CONCISE LAW**

If you're reading this, then more than likely you're in prison. One of the hardest things to find in prison is relevant case law, rules and statutes. It's almost impossible for an inmate to cite up-to-date case law—most lawyers don't even cite up-to-date case law.

Having said that, it is important for you to cite relevant case law. And this isn't the case law that you get from legal beagles on the yard that use the same case law for each and every petition. Relevant case law is case law that goes to the heart of your issue. Relevant case law is not general "due process" or "violation of rights" case law—that's going to apply to every claim that is made, generally.

You need to cite case law that addresses the exact issue you are arguing. So if you are arguing that the jury didn't find an aggravating factor that is also part of the element of the offense, find a case that addresses that issue.
How do you find that case? See, Section C(3). The best practice is to write to your advisory counsel and explain what your exact issue is and then ask if they could send you a case or two that covers that issue. With a specific request, your advisory counsel should send you a couple of cases.

9. **WHAT'S YOUR POINT? (ANALYSIS OF HOW YOUR FACTS FIT THE LAW)**

In law school, all students are taught the IRAC method of legal writing. The acronym stands for Issue, Rule, Analysis and Conclusion. You should utilize that method when writing your pro se petition arguments. So after you have drafted your statement of facts, the statement of facts within your personal knowledge you will begin your argument section. Within that section is where you will utilize the IRAC method.

i. Details on How to Use the IRAC Method

First, you identify the **issue** that you want address. The issue will be stated something to the effective of, "[Attorney Name] provided ineffective assistance of counsel by failing to properly cross-examine a key witness with respect to the witness's reliability when the attorney failed to address the witnesses criminal record." That opening sentence lets the reader know exactly what your issue is and what is going to be addressed in that specific section.

[See Section L(4)(iii) for a detailed discussion on how to draft a persuasive issue.]

After you identify the issue, then you'll explain the **rule** (or case law) that will control your issue. In most petitions, the case law will be regarding ineffective assistance of counsel. That law is contained in the sample petition provided with this manual. **(See, Form #5—*Sample Petition For Post-Conviction Relief*)**

If you are not raising an ineffective assistance of counsel claim, make sure you cite relevant case law that corresponds to your issue. Again, do not cite generic "due process" law for your issue.

The third part of your argument will be the **analysis** portion. This is the meat of your petition and where you need to convince the judge that you are either entitled to an evidentiary hearing or entitled to the relief you are seeking.

CRITICAL TIP: In the analysis portion of your argument you will write out the most important facts that support your issue. You need to tell the story of your case and then weave the law that you previously cited back into the argument that you are making with the facts you are using. While this section is the most important section of your petition, make sure to be concise—don't write too much because the reader will start to skim your argument instead of reading it as careful as you would want them to.

The final part of your petition will be the **conclusion**. While some think the conclusion is just an afterthought and not important—they are incorrect. Use the conclusion effectively—tell the judge exactly what you want. Don't just state, "Petitioner requests whatever relief is proper under the law," or something to that effect. Instead, tell the judge that you want findings of fact that the attorney provided ineffective assistance of counsel, or that you want to keep the plea agreement in tact but are requesting to be resentenced. Remember: keep in clear and concise, the judge will appreciate it. But most importantly, be specific about the exact relief you are seeking.

10. **FEDERALIZING YOUR PETITION**

When you file your petition for post-conviction relief, you'll file it in State court. First at the Superior Court level, then if the petition is denied, you'll file with the Arizona Court of Appeals and then the Arizona Supreme Court. If you are unsuccessful at each stage, then the next option available to you is to file a Petition for a Writ of Habeas Corpus in federal district court.

i. Exhaustion in State Court

Before filing in federal court, however, you must file a petition for review with the higher courts (Arizona Court of Appeals and Arizona Supreme Court). That is called "exhaustion." You must "exhaust" or present your case to every available State court prior to proceeding to federal court.

Filing a petition for review with the Court of Appeals in non-death penalty cases is sufficient to satisfy the exhaustion requirements in federal court. That means you don't have to file a petition for review with the Arizona Supreme Court in order to fulfill the exhaustion requirement prior to filing a petition for a writ of habeas corpus in federal court.

The petition for review with the Arizona Supreme Court is discretionary (you can do it or not without a consequence to your federal case) but you may want to file just to get another opportunity for relief in your case.

ii. How to Federalize Your Petition

You'll only be able to file in federal court if you have federal issues for the federal court to address. That means you have to raise those federal issues in your original petition for post-conviction relief that you filed in Superior Court in Arizona.

So when you hear of "federalizing your petition," it means to write your petition in such a way that, if you lose at the State level, you will not be precluded (stopped) from raising your issues in federal court.

CRITICAL TIP: To federalize your petition you must cite to and argue federal law as it pertains to the issues in your petition. If you do not cite and argue federal law in your petition, then any action you file in federal court will be dismissed. The reason the federal action will ultimately be dismissed is because you did not give the State court an opportunity to rule on the federal issues. The federal court will not review any issue that was not considered and ruled on by the state court.

And it is not sufficient enough for you to cite the United States Constitution—you must cite, discuss and argue the appropriate federal law, whether it's the U.S. Constitution, federal statute and/or federal case law. And then after you cite the federal law, you then have to give a proper analysis of why the federal law applies to your case and why you are entitled to relief under the federal law.

Most issues raised in petitions for post-conviction relief are ineffective assistance of counsel claims. Those claims are typically federalized because the leading case for those claims is *Strickland v. Washington*, 466 U.S. 668 (1984). Most defendants know the *Strickland* case and will cite to it. The *Strickland* case is a federal case (decided by the United States Supreme Court) and is sufficient to federalize your petition. You should also cite to the 5th, 6th and 14th Amendments of the United States Constitution, as they apply to the right to effective counsel. **[See, Section N for the federal law controlling this issue.]**

The above example would only apply to ineffective assistance of counsel claims. If you have a different claim other than an ineffective assistance of counsel claim, then you are required to find the federal law that applies to your specific claim and argue that law in your petition.

For example, if you are arguing that the State of Arizona breached your plea agreement (for whatever reason), then you would cite the Arizona cases along with the federal cases (*Santobello v. New York*, 423 U.S. 61 (1975), *Blackledge v. Perry*, 417 U.S. 21 (1974)). If you only cite the Arizona cases (and not the federal cases), then when you file in federal court, the federal court will deny your petition (a procedural default) because you failed to raise the federal issue in your State court petition for post-conviction relief.

CRITICAL TIP: And you must raise the federal issue in your original petition for post-conviction relief AND your petition for review with the Arizona Court of Appeals (and Arizona Supreme Court, if you choose to file with the AZ Supreme Court). It is insufficient to cite and argue the federal issues only in your petition for review.

iii. Which Federal Court To File In?

There are four federal courts in Arizona (it's actually called "the District of Arizona" with respect to federal court). You will have to file your case with the correct federal court, which depends on the county in which you were convicted and sentenced.

If you were convicted and sentenced in the following counties, then you are required to file in the Phoenix Division of the District of Arizona: Maricopa, Pinal, Yuma, La Paz and Gila.

If you were convicted and sentenced in the following counties, then you are required to file in the Tucson Division of the District of Arizona: Pima, Cochise, Santa Cruz, Graham and Greenlee.

If you were convicted and sentenced in the following counties, then you are required to file in the Prescott Division of the District of Arizona: Apache, Navajo, Coconino, Mohave and Yavapai. **NOTE: If your case arises out of one of the following five counties in the Prescott Division, then you should file in the Phoenix Division.**

Here are the addresses of the two federal courts you need to file your Petition for Writ of Habeas Corpus:

Phoenix:
Sandra Day O'Connor United States Courthouse
401 W. Washington St., Suite 130, SPC 1
Phoenix, Arizona 85003
(602) 322-7200
Tucson:
Evo A. DeConcini United States Courthouse
405 W. Congress Street, Suite 1500
Tucson, Arizona 85701
(520) 205-4200

The instructions and forms for filing a pro se petition for a writ of habeas corpus should be available at the prison. Ask your counselor (COIII) for the packet provided by the District Court of Arizona. If he or she does not have the packet, it can be found at: www.azd.uscourts.gov/forms.

It is extremely difficult to properly fill out and have the district court accept your pro se petition. The instructions that come with the forms in the packet should be sufficient to properly fill out and file your petition for a writ of habeas corpus.

11. BURDENS OF PROOF FOR YOU AND THE STATE

The first hurdle to get over with respect to your petition for post-conviction relief is for the court to grant an evidentiary hearing on the issues that you raised in your petition. Once you are granted an evidentiary hearing, then it will be up to you to prove your case.

Pursuant to **Rule 32.8(c)**, you will have the burden of proof to prove the allegations of fact by a preponderance of the evidence. That burden is relatively low to prove—it's a simple standard of "more likely than not." Some call this burden "51%."

Once you meet your burden of proof, then the burden shifts to the State to prove that the error you proved was harmless beyond a reasonable doubt. The beyond a reasonable doubt standard is the highest standard in our entire court system and is exceptionally difficult to meet.

For details about how to conduct an evidentiary hearing, see Section K.

12. DECLARATION

When you file a petition for post-conviction relief, you must also file a declaration along with the petition. **(See, Form #6—*Declaration*)** The declaration is required by **Rule 32.5** and is a relatively simple document that states you are putting forth all claims known to you at this time.

[Rule 32.5: "The petition shall be accompanied by a declaration by the defendant stating under penalty of perjury that the information contained is true to the best of the defendant's knowledge and belief."]

The reason the rules require the declaration is because under Rule 32 you have to present all known claims in the first petition you file. You can't have a few claims that you want to raise now and do them one at a time to see if one is successful.

CRITICAL TIP: If you don't raise an issue in your first petition, then that issue is waived—you won't be able to raise it in a later petition.

The declaration you sign says that you are raising every known issue in the first petition and are not leaving out any issues.

I. DRAFTING LEGAL ARGUMENTS

Now that you have a strong statement of facts and prepared the statement of facts within the defendant's knowledge, the next section to draft is your actual legal arguments. This is the part of the petition where you analyze the facts of your case with the relevant case law and show how you are entitled to relief under Rule 32. See Section H(9)(i) for detailed instructions on how to properly write an argument using the IRAC formula.

[See, APPENDIX A for case law synopses regarding various aspects of Rule 32.]

In the "Discussion" section or "Legal Arguments" section of your petition you need to identify your exact issue—a general "violation of due process" argument is weak and will not get your relief. Pinpoint exactly what went wrong in your case legally and cite to that case law and/or statute and/or rule of criminal procedure. Develop the case law/statute/rule to show how it is good standing law and relevant to your case.

CRITICAL TIP: If there are competing cases, explain those cases in your petition—acting like cases that hurt your position don't exist will do nothing to help your case. The prosecutor will be using any and all cases that contradict your position so the better practice is to get in front of the prosecutor by raising the contradicting case law and highlighting how that case is inapplicable to your case.

Once you have developed the law, pull out the relevant facts of your case and show how those facts support the legal conclusion that you are requesting. In other words, argue the following: "X, Y & Z facts supported a finding of ineffective assistance of counsel in Sample v. State, and in my case X, Y & Z facts are also present, and as such, my attorney provided ineffective assistance of counsel."

Again, for a more detailed and exhaustive explanation on drafting and crafting your legal arguments, see Section H(9)(i).

J. NEEDING MORE TIME (MOTIONS TO EXTEND TIME)

After your attorney files a Notice of Completion, the judge will give you approximately 40 days to file a pro per petition for post-conviction relief. Inevitably, you will need more than the initial 40 days to file your petition. It will take a while just to receive the materials from your attorney, and then if you need additional documents or need to locate a witness, etc., then you'll need even more time. This section will show you how to request additional time to file your pro per petition for post-conviction relief.

1. EXTENDING TIME VS. STAYS VS. DISMISSAL WITHOUT PREJUDICE

This section will explain the difference between Motions to Extend Time, Stays and Dismissals, and will explain the best practices to use to have the best chance at getting each one granted. All three legal requests are different and serve distinct purposes.

i. Extending Time to File the Pro Per Petition

A motion to extend time is a pleading where you are asking the judge to give you more time to file the pro per petition for post-conviction relief. Motions to extend time are the most frequently filed motions in Rule 32 proceedings. **(See, Form #7—*Motion to Extend Time*)**

Judges routinely grant the first motion to extend time that you file. As long as you present a legitimate basis for needing more time to prepare your petition, the judge will grant the motion. The most commonly used reasons for needing more time by pro per litigants in Rule 32 proceedings is the lack of resources at the prison, needing more time to communicate with advisory counsel, needing more time to gather relevant documents and needing more time to prepare the pro per petition. Be sure to cite the fact that you are in prison with limited resources to prepare your petition in your motion (if, in fact, that is what is causing you to need more time).

On average, pro per litigants request 2-3 extension of time to file their petition, which is equivalent to 100-130 days to prepare and file your petition.

CRITICAL TIP: Make sure to file (mail) your motion to extend time a week prior to the due date. If you wait until the due date or after the due date, you take the chance of the judge dismissing your Rule 32 proceedings because of your late request.

ii. Request to Stay the Rule 32 Proceedings

A "stay" is when you want the Rule 32 proceedings to proceed but not on the court's active calendar. Stays are usually requested when a certain event is likely to occur in the near future. **(See, Forms #8a & 8b—*Sample Motion to Stay Rule 32 Proceedings & Motion to Stay Rule 32 Proceedings Form*)**

For example, assume a defendant accepted a plea agreement and then was sentenced. Following sentencing, the defendant filed a motion for a specific reason. At the same time as filing the post-sentencing motion, the defendant filed his Notice of Post-Conviction Relief, which started his Rule 32 proceedings. The judge is going to set a due date for his petition for post-conviction relief, but if he wants the motion ruled on first, he may need to file a request for a stay.

When you file a stay, you have to identify the specific event that you want to stay your Rule 32 proceedings until. So in the above example, you would request a stay until the judge ruled on the post-sentencing motion.

Stays were commonplace for cases that were still pending on appeal but, for whatever reason, the Rule 32 proceedings had started prior to the final decision by the Court of Appeals and/or the Arizona Supreme Court. Now, the courts prefer that you request a dismissal of your case, pending appeal.

iii. Motion to Dismiss the Rule 32 Proceedings

A motion to dismiss is a request that your Rule 32 proceedings be taken off the active calendar and that all due dates for the petition for post-conviction relief be vacated. **(See, Forms #9a & 9b—*Sample Motion to Dismiss Rule 32 Proceedings & Motion to Dismiss Rule 32 Proceedings Form*)**

A motion to dismiss can be made "with prejudice" or "without prejudice." With prejudice means that you want the case dismissed for good, it will never come back. Those are extremely rare and almost never a good idea.

A motion to dismiss without prejudice means that you can re-file your Notice of Post-Conviction Relief to start your Rule 32 proceedings up again at a later date. Just like with the Request for Stay, you must identify the specific event that is causing you to file the motion to dismiss without prejudice. A defendant's case pending on appeal is the most frequently cited basis for filing a motion to dismiss without prejudice.

CRITICAL TIP: When the judge grants the motion to dismiss without prejudice, a timeline or deadline is always set in the judge's order, which is controlled by a triggering event. The order will indicate something to the effect, "The case is dismissed without prejudice and the defendant may re-file a Notice of Post-Conviction Relief within 30 days of the Court of Appeals filing its mandate." The triggering event in this example is the Court of Appeals filing a mandate. Be sure to re-file a Notice of Post-Conviction Relief by whatever deadline is set. If your appellate attorney fails to send you the Court of Appeals' decision/mandate, you may file your Notice of Post-Conviction Relief late and explain the reasons for doing so. See, Section B(1) discussing Rule 32.1(f).

The difference between a Stay and a Motion to Dismiss Without Prejudice is the judge will stay the proceedings on the active calendar for a certain number of days or until a certain event. The Motion to Dismiss allows the case to drop off of the active calendar and requires the defendant to re-file a Notice of Post-Conviction Relief to start the Rule 32 proceedings up again. Stays are less frequently done, while Motions to Dismiss Without Prejudice are routine.

2. **MOTION TO EXPAND THE RECORD – REQUEST FOR PREPARATION OF TRANSCRIPTS**

Once you receive the trial file, transcripts and record on appeal (if you had an appeal following a trial), you may find that you need additional transcripts. Sections E & F discuss in detail what materials you are supposed to get and from whom.

If after receiving all of your transcripts you feel that you need more transcripts (transcripts are the word-for-word record of what was said during a court proceedings), then you need to make the correct request to obtain those transcripts. With an appeal before the Court of Appeals, you would go directly to the court and file a Motion to Expand the Record. The "expand" means to add to the record. You would be requesting to add a transcript to the record.

When requesting a transcript for your Rule 32 case, you have to first get permission from the contracting agency (Office of Court Appointed Counsel in Pima County or Office of Public Defense Services in Maricopa County, or the Court Administration in all other counties) to get the money for the preparation of the transcript. Each agency has a form to use in order to request the preparation of the transcript. You (or your advisory counsel or family member) print out the form, fill it out and mail it in to the agency. **(See, Forms #10 & #11** *– Request for Expenditure of Funds***)**

Office of Public Defense Services
620 W. Jackson St., Suite 3076
Phoenix, Arizona 85003
(*For Maricopa County Cases*)

Office of Court-Appointed Counsel
33 N. Stone Ave., 19th Floor
Tucson, Arizona 85001
(*For Pima County Cases*)

If your case is not in Maricopa or Pima county, then you should contact the court administrator regarding the expenses to prepare the transcript you need. See, Section B(2) for the court addresses. Indicate on the front of the envelope that the letter is for the "Court Administrator."

Once you have permission to have the transcript produced, then you contact the court reporter who transcribed the hearing. You can find out who the court reporter is by looking on the minute entry of the hearing that you want transcribed—his or her name will be listed on the minute entry. If the hearing was recorded with a digital recording device, then you must go to the managing court reporter to have the hearing transcribed.

Your advisory counsel should do all of this for you but if not, you can contact the court reporter by sending a letter to the court that your case originated from. See, Section B(2).

You can file a request to stay the Rule 32 proceedings until you have received the transcript, at which time you would have to file a Notice of Receipt of Transcript and ask that a due date for your pro per petition for post-conviction relief be re-set.

K. EVIDENTIARY HEARING

Many inmates ask, "When do I go back to court on my case?" when I first speak to them. They are wondering when they can get a court date with the judge to explain their arguments. Rule 32 cases rarely go back into court. And when they do make it back into the courtroom, it is almost always for an evidentiary hearing.

Rule 32.8 controls the evidentiary hearing. Rule 32.8 states that you "shall be entitled to a hearing to determine issues of material fact..." That language makes it sound as though every defendant who files a Rule 32 petition gets an evidentiary hearing. That is not the case. Approximately 10% of defendants who file a petition for post-conviction relief are granted an evidentiary hearing.

The court uses evidentiary hearings to take testimony and receive evidence regarding the facts and issues raised in your petition—and only when the petition for post-conviction relief has put forth compelling and convincing arguments that show relief is more likely than not warranted.

THE MOST CRITICAL TIP: If your pro per petition for post-conviction relief is granted and you are allowed to withdraw from your plea agreement or your granted a new trial, then you will be subject to a longer prison sentence. That doesn't mean you'll get a longer prison sentence, but it is a possibility. It is also a possibility that you will receive a shorter prison sentence. Of course the main goal is to get the case dismissed, but if you proceed with a petition for post-conviction relief, you need to know that you are subjecting yourself to a potentially longer prison sentence.

1. REQUESTING NEW COUNSEL FOR AN EVIDENTIARY HEARING

Some judges will expect you to conduct the entire evidentiary hearing (call and cross-examine witnesses, give closing arguments, etc.) and some will expect your advisory counsel to conduct the hearing. Knowing which one is expected at your hearing is essential.

CRITICAL TIP: File a request for clarification with the judge who granted the evidentiary hearing and ask who (you or advisory counsel) will be expected to conduct the hearing.

If you received an evidentiary hearing by filing a pro per petition, that means your advisory counsel has already gave his or her opinion that your issue has no merit. Do you really want an attorney arguing your case in court who feels your issue(s) has no merit?

If your advisory counsel is expected to present the case at an evidentiary hearing, then you should request new advisory counsel. First, you should write to your current advisory counsel (the one who filed the original notice with the court indicating that no issues were present in your case) and ask them to file a motion to withdraw/substitute counsel based on the conflict of interest. The conflict of interest is the advisory counsel presenting an issue in court that he or she has already said has no merit. Most of the time, the advisory counsel will file the motion and new counsel will be appointed.

CRITICAL TIP: If your advisory counsel does not file the motion to withdraw/substitute counsel, then you should file it with the court and ask the judge to appoint new advisory counsel based on the obvious conflict of interest.

Ethical Rule 3.1 states, "What is required of lawyers...is that they inform themselves about the facts of their clients' cases and the applicable law and determine that they can make good faith and nonfrivolous arguments in support of their clients' positions." E.R., 3.1, Comment 2.

If your advisory counsel cannot make the good faith argument required by E.R. 3.1 in court, then they should withdraw.

2. **INEFFECTIVE ASSISTANCE OF CLIENT (YES, *CLIENT*)**

If your advisory counsel will be conducting the hearing, then it is important you communicate with him or her prior to the hearing.

The judge will set the hearing out approximately 45 to 60 days, which will give you sufficient time to speak with your advisory counsel and coordinate which evidence, witnesses, etc. will be presented at the hearing. If you rely solely upon advisory counsel to prepare for the hearing, then you have provided "ineffective assistance" to your advisory counsel. No one cares about your case as much as you do—make sure to stay in contact with your advisory counsel and know exactly what will be done (in terms of evidence and argument) at your evidentiary hearing.

You will still be at the prison when your evidentiary hearing is set and will be moved to the jail of the county where your hearing will take place. While at the prison, you should arrange legal calls with your advisory counsel to begin the planning process for your evidentiary hearing. Once you are moved to the jail—which will be anywhere from a week to a couple of days before the hearing—then you can meet with your advisory counsel face-to-face to finalize your strategy for the hearing.

Prior to being moved from the prison to the jail, you should copy and mail to your advisory counsel all of the documents you want to use at the evidentiary hearing as exhibits. You should also bring a copy of those documents/exhibits with you when you are moved to the jail. Do not rely on your advisory counsel.

You should also inform your advisory counsel which witnesses you will want to call to testify at the evidentiary hearing and a list of questions you want asked of each witness.

3. **WHAT HAPPENS AT THE HEARING**

Now that you are prepared, have a strategy, your exhibits and argument ready, it's time to conduct the hearing. An evidentiary hearing under Rule 32 is conducted similar to a criminal trial, except that you may be called to testify. In a criminal trial, a defendant does not have to testify, but in Rule 32 hearings, you can be called by the State to testify.

The format of the evidentiary hearing is as follows: the parties give opening statements, the defendant calls witnesses, the State calls witnesses, the defendant may call rebuttal witnesses (witnesses who rebut or disprove what the State's witnesses testified to) and then the parties give closing arguments. After the hearing, the judge will typically take the matter "under advisement," which means that he or she will issue a written decision at a later date.

4. ADDRESSING THE COURT

When speaking in court make sure to show respect for the court by addressing the judge as "your honor" or "judge," never by their name. Every word you say will be recorded by a court reporter or digital recording device so be sure to speak loudly and clearly. When referring to the prosecutor, you can call them by their last name, "Mr. or Mrs. X," or simply call them "the State."

5. GETTING WITNESSES TO COURT

As detailed in Section F(1), you have subpoena power during your Rule 32 proceedings. With respect to the evidentiary hearing, you should subpoena each witness you intend to call at the hearing.

CRITICAL TIP: If you do not subpoena the witnesses, then they may not show up. Subpoenaing the witnesses makes it binding on the witness that they show up for the hearing or else they will be violating a court order (the subpoena) and the court can issue sanctions against that person. Without a subpoena, you are just hoping the witness shows up.

Your advisory counsel should subpoena witnesses on your behalf. Make sure to communicate frequently (in writing) with your advisory counsel about which witnesses will be subpoenaed and ask for proof that the witnesses were served with a subpoena.

6. ASKING WITNESSES QUESTIONS

There are three types of testimony you will take from witnesses who are called to testify at your evidentiary hearing: Direct, Cross-Examination and Redirect. Direct testimony is when you call the witness to the witness stand (as opposed to the State calling the witness) and are the first person to ask the witness questions. Cross-Examination testimony is when you are the person to ask the witness questions second. And Redirect testimony comes after cross-examination testimony and is asked by the person who initially called the witness to testify.

With Direct testimony you are asking the witness to paint a picture for the judge about whatever issue you are raising. You cannot "lead" a witness with your questions, which means you cannot suggest an answer in your question. For example, you cannot ask on direct examination: "Isn't it true that I told my lawyer that I wanted to accept the plea agreement?" That is a leading question that will be objected to by the prosecutor. You would have to ask something like, "Do you know what I told my lawyer about accepting a plea agreement?" In other words, you cannot ask "yes or no" questions with direct testimony.

Direct testimony can be harder to take than cross-examination testimony because with cross-examination testimony you can (and should) ask "yes or no" questions. With cross-examination testimony, you want to lead the witness right to the answer you want with your questions without the witness giving a narrative (long story) for their answer. And you never (or hardly ever) want to ask the question, "why?" This question opens the door for the witness to say whatever they want and explain their actions or inactions however they way. Most cross-examination questions begin with, "Isn't it true..."

CRITICAL TIP: Witnesses who you are cross-examining are against your position and do not want to help you out at all. You have to be careful of the questions you are asking them and only ask questions you know the answers to.

The party who initially called the witness to the stand takes redirect testimony. Redirect testimony is optional and is only used to clarify answers given on cross-examination. Redirect testimony must be limited to the answers/issues raised on cross-examination.

7. **BURDENS OF PROOF (YOURS AND THE STATE'S)**

There are several different burdens of proof in criminal law: reasonable suspicion, probable cause, preponderance of the evidence, clear and convincing evidence and beyond a reasonable doubt.

If you are granted an evidentiary hearing, then you have to prove the facts/issues in your petition by a preponderance of the evidence—that's called the burden of proof. Your burden is preponderance of the evidence. The preponderance of the evidence burden means you have to prove your facts/issues "more likely than not" to the judge. It is not a difficult burden to sustain, often referred to as 51%.

If, by the witnesses you call and evidence you present at the evidentiary hearing, you meet that burden of proof, then Rule 32.8(c) requires the State to prove that the error or defect you proved in your case was harmless "beyond a reasonable doubt." So once you meet your burden and prove your case, the State has the opportunity to show that the error was harmless. But in order to do so, the State has to meet the highest burden in our legal system: beyond a reasonable doubt.

So when you are at your evidentiary hearing, be prepared to not only prove your case and clearly show the error in your case, but also be prepared to argue why that error is not a harmless error.

Harmless error is an error that occurred but if the judge was to fix the error the result of the trial or proceeding would remain the same. In other words, harmless error is like saying, "Yes there was a problem with your proceedings but even without that problem, the result would have been the exact same."

8. **WAS THAT YOUR CLOSING ARGUMENT!?**

After presenting all of your witnesses and evidence, the judge will ask if you wish to give a closing statement or closing argument. The closing argument is optional and is used to sum up what your evidence showed during the hearing. Because evidentiary hearings are presented to a judge, closing arguments should be brief—the judge has already read your issue in your pleadings and heard the testimony and considered the evidence at the hearing.

A closing argument at an evidentiary hearing is a good time to tell the judge exactly what you want (the relief sought) and why he or she should grant that relief.

CRITICAL TIP: Following closing arguments, you should request that the judge issue an order directing that you be returned to the Arizona Department of Corrections immediately. If you do not get that order, you could spend several weeks at the county jail. If you wish to remain at the jail, then do not request the order and hope that the sheriff's office does not move you immediately. Most defendants want to return to prison as soon as possible, however, so the return order should be requested at the evidentiary hearing.

9. **COURT'S DECISION**

According to Rule 32.8(d), the judge's decision is supposed to be made within 10 days of the date of the evidentiary hearing. Rule 32.8(d) also allows the judge to take longer in "extraordinary circumstances." The ruling typically is done within 30 days of the hearing.

If you receive a decision that gives factual and legal analysis but denies your petition, go to Section L.

CRITICAL TIP: If the judge denies your petition for post-conviction relief with a one or two sentence minute entry without giving any factual or legal analysis, then you should file a Request for Findings of Fact and Conclusions of Law. Findings of Fact and Conclusions of Law are when a judge gives a full explanation of why and how he or she reached their decision. If you fail to get a full explanation from the court as to how the final decision was reached, then your case will be handicapped for the review process.

If the judge issues a one or two sentence ruling denying your petition for post-conviction relief, and you file a petition for review with the Arizona Court of Appeals, the Court of Appeals will assume that the trial court used sound legal reasoning and affirm your conviction and sentence. If you do not get detailed factual findings and legal analysis from the judge who heard the evidentiary hearing, then you will not be able to explain to the Court of Appeals the errors made by the evidentiary hearing judge's decision.

In *State v. Moody*, 208 Ariz. 424, ¶ 81, 94 P.3d 1119, 1144 (2004), the court stated "we presume that the court was aware of the relevant law and applied it correctly..." You want to avoid having the Court of Appeals have this weapon at their disposal for your case. To take it away, you have to get the Rule 32 judge to explain his or her decision so that no assumptions will be made regarding whether the law/facts were applied correctly.

L. **MOTION FOR REHEARING/PETITION FOR REVIEW**

A motion for rehearing is filed after you receive the trial court's decision denying your petition for post-conviction relief. See, Rule 32.9(a). The motion for rehearing serves as a mini appeal back to the same judge who just issued the ruling. As such, it is rare that a motion for rehearing will ever be granted. In fact, the State is not even supposed to file a response to any motion for rehearing unless ordered to do so by the judge. A motion for rehearing must be filed within 15 days of the trial court's ruling on your petition for post-conviction relief.

A petition for review is filed with the Arizona Court of Appeals and asks the Court of Appeals to review the trial court's ruling and to remand the case back to the trial court because of errors made by the trial court. **(See, Form #12 – *Sample Petition for Review*)**

A petition for review comes only after a denial of a petition for post-conviction relief and must be filed within 30 days of the trial court's ruling on your petition for post-conviction relief or motion for rehearing.

1. **WHICH COURT IS THE CORRECT COURT?**

   There are two Courts of Appeal in Arizona: Division One and Division Two. Division One is located in Phoenix and Division Two is located in Tucson.

   Division One decides cases that stem from the following counties: Apache, Coconino, La Paz, Navajo, Maricopa, Mohave, Yavapai and Yuma.

   Division Two decides cases that originate from the following counties: Cochise, Gila, Graham, Greenlee, Pima, Pinal and Santa Cruz.

   Find which county your case originated from and file your petition for review with the correct Court of Appeals.

   Court of Appeals – Division One
   Attn: Clerk of the Court
   1501 W. Washington Street
   Phoenix, Arizona 85007
   Phone: (602)542-4821

   Court of Appeals – Division Two
   Attn: Clerk of the Court
   400 W. Congress Street
   Tucson, Arizona 85701
   Phone: (520) 628-6954

   No matter which Court of Appeals you file your petition for review in, the Court of Appeals has a policy that Division Two will ultimately decide all petitions for review that are filed as a result of a denial of a petition for post-conviction relief. You still have to file in the correct court (either Division One or Division Two), but once it is time to decide your petition for review, Division Two will be issuing the ruling. So if you file a petition for review with Division One, after a few weeks or months, you will get a notice indicating that your case was transferred to Division Two for a ruling.

2. **TIMELINES REGARDING PETITIONS FOR REVIEW**

   You must file your petition for review with the Court of Appeals within thirty (30) days of the trial court's decision denying your petition for post-conviction relief. Rule 32.9(c) indicates that the petition for review must be filed "within thirty days after the final decision of the trial court." The words "final decision" could mean two different dates.

The rule does not indicate which date is controlling: the date on the ruling or the date the ruling is filed with the clerk—most of the time those dates are different. In any event, you should error on the side of caution and file your petition for review with the Court of Appeals within thirty days of the date of the ruling, not the file date.

If you need more time to file the petition for review, you send in a motion for an extension of time to file the petition for review with the Superior Court that ruled on your case. See, Section B(b) for the court addresses. As is the case with motions to extend time to file your pro per petition for post-conviction relief, motions to extend time to file your petition for review with the Court of Appeals are routinely granted. Just make sure you do not abuse the leniency of the court by requesting multiple extensions to file—one or two should be sufficient to file your petition.

3. **WHICH ISSUES ARE THE CORRECT ISSUES TO RAISE?**

The Court of Appeals has issued a ruling that explains they only want to consider two or three of your strongest issues—anything beyond that (in a non-death penalty case) is overkill and seen as you being desperate to have an issue. Many pro pers want to raise as many issues as they can in their briefs, but the Court of Appeals has explained that the better practice is to pick two or three of your strongest issues and raise those. There is a better chance your entire brief gets read thoroughly (rather than being skimmed) if you raise two or three strong issues.

The strongest issues to raise are issues that will affect defendants across the entire State of Arizona, not just something specific to your case. It's rare that such an issue presents itself for review in a case, so if you have one be sure to raise it. Those types of issues are sentencing issues that affect all defendants, illegal statutes, defects in procedural rules, etc.

While you may not have an issue that affects defendants across the entire State, you still will have to parse out what are your strongest issues. Avoid, if you can, the issues that rely on an abuse of discretion of the trial court. The Court of Appeals gives great deference to the trial court when it comes to discretion. Instead, focus on issues that would amount to structural error (error that is so egregious that the judge's discretion does not play a part in the issue).

4. **FORMAT OF PETITION FOR REVIEW**

The Court of Appeals does not require pleading paper. In fact, the Court of Appeals does not want you to use pleading paper, only white paper.

The difference with the Court of Appeals is that they want you to number each of your paragraphs, whereas the trial court does not. You should also cite to the specific pages of your pro per petition for post-conviction relief when referring to your previous arguments. In addition, you should cite to, and attach to your petition for review, any important documents that support the points you raise.

It is mandatory that you attach a copy of the trial court's ruling from which you are filing the petition for review. In other words, the Court of Appeals wants to see what you are challenging. Be sure to cite to the specific page of the decisions in the trial court's ruling that you are challenging.

i. *Caption Page*

The caption page to the petition for review with the Court of Appeals is the same as the caption for your pro per petition for review with just a few minor, but important, changes.

First, you need to change the court's name to the Arizona Court of Appeals. Underneath "Arizona Court of Appeals" should be either "Division One" or "Division Two" depending on which division you are filing in.

Unlike pleadings filed in Superior Court, pleadings filed in the Court of Appeals do not need to have the numbers 1-28 down the left-hand side of the page.

The title of your document will be "Petition for Review." Underneath "Petition for Review" should be the words "Denial of Petition for Post-Conviction Relief." Those words let the Court of Appeals know why the petition for review is being filed.

Finally, the names of the parties change. You go from being a defendant in Superior Court to being a Petitioner in the Court of Appeals. The State of Arizona still is on top in the caption, but it should be listed as "Respondent." Your name is below the "vs." and should be listed as "Petitioner."

ii. *Statement of Material Facts*

The first section of your petition for review will be a statement of facts. I label this section "Statement of Material Facts," it could also be termed "Statement of Relevant Facts."

The facts you recited in your pro per petition for post-conviction relief may be sufficient for your petition for review, they may not be. It depends on the issue(s) you are raising in your petition for review.

You should only put facts in that are "material." In other words, you should only write down relevant facts that play a key part in the issue.

For example, if you are challenging a certain procedural rule, the details of your crime may be irrelevant. On the other hand, if you are challenging the evidence used against you, the facts relating to the commission of the crime may be highly relevant.

CRITICAL TIP: Be sure to only put forth facts that will help the judges make a decision on your issue—anything else is just fat that needs to be trimmed off.

CRITICAL TIP: In your statement of facts, include the details of what happened in the trial court with respect to your pro per petition for post-conviction relief. Explain when you filed, when the trial court ruled, how the trial court ruled and how your petition for review is timely. This will be the last paragraph in your Statement of Material Facts.

iii. Presentation of Your Issues

The second section of the petition for review is designated "Issues Presented for Review." Here is where you will inform the Court of Appeals about the specific issues that you will be discussing within your petition. Presenting your issues may seem like a relatively simple task, it can be one of the most daunting tasks in writing the petition for review.

Typically, you will begin your issue with the phrase, "Whether the trial court erred..." Immediately following those words, you will write out how the trial court made a mistake, such as ..."in finding that the newly discovered evidence did not exist before trial."

CRITICAL TIP: It is important to give details when presenting your issue. Make sure to expound on the facts of the issue and weave in the trial court's findings.

The following is an example of one issue written three different ways:

BAD: Whether the trial court erred in finding that newly discovered evidence did not exist before trial.

BETTER: Whether the trial court erred in finding that the eyewitness's testimony did not constitute newly discovered evidence when it did not exist before trial.

BEST: Whether the trial court erred in finding that the eyewitness's testimony did not constitute newly discovered evidence when the witness, after diligent efforts by trial counsel, was not able to be located prior to trial, was located after trial and presented an affidavit as to what his testimony would have been at trial.

You want to make the statement of your issue compelling—it's the first thing some judges flip to when they begin to read your petition for review. You want to plant a strong seed in their mind while they are reading your issue that you have a legitimate claim. If you write a strong issue, then the judge will be reading your petition with your issue in mind and not searching for the issue while reading through your argument.

iv. Procedural History of Entire Case

The procedural history of your is when pleadings were filed, when the case was filed, if it was dismissed, when you were found guilty, when you were sentenced, if you were re-sentenced, etc. The procedural history is not related to the facts of the crime, only what took place in court.

The procedural history section of your petition for review is optional and should only be used if your case has a peculiar procedural history. If you feel you need to explain to the Court of Appeals the procedural history of your case and how you got to the Court of Appeals, do so. If your case is relatively straight forward (Indictment, Plea Agreement or Trial, Sentencing, Appeal/Rule 32, Petition for Review), then it is not necessary.

v. *Discussion/Argument Section*

The discussion or argument section (you can label this section either discussion or argument) is the meat of your petition. The discussion section is where you argue why your petition for review should be granted.

CRITICAL TIP: Remember that you are complaining to the Court of Appeals about the Superior Court's decision, not your issue. In other words, do not re-argue, by cutting and pasting, the issues you argued in your petition for post-conviction relief in your petition for review. Instead, argue why the Superior Court erred in making its decision.

The discussion section should focus on the trial court's reasoning when deciding your issue. You will want to break down the trial court's reasoning and show how it is flawed. Do not simply cut-and-paste the argument you raised in your petition for post-conviction relief. The Court of Appeals does everything it can to affirm the lower courts—you have to detail how the lower court made the wrong decision, not that you have a legitimate issue.

Of course you will want to explain your issue to the Court of Appeals, but do so in the context of how the trial court erred in reaching its decision to deny your petition for post-conviction relief.

CRITICAL TIP: Because you need to thoroughly examine the trial court's findings and how those findings were wrong, it is vital to make sure the trial court explains itself when writing the decision denying your pro per petition for post-conviction relief. As stated in Section K(9), be sure to request Findings of Fact and Conclusions of Law from the trial court. The better practice is to request the Findings of Fact and Conclusions of Law prior to the judge issuing a decision on your pro per petition for post-conviction relief. But if the judge has already issued a decision on your case and it is a short (two or three sentence) decision with no explanation, then file a Request for Findings of Fact and Conclusions of Law requesting a detailed explanation of the judge's decision. Without that detailed explanation, the Court of Appeals will "presume that the court was aware of the relevant law and applied it correctly..." *State v. Moody*, 208 Ariz. 424, ¶ 81, 94 P.3d 1119, 1144 (2004).

vi. *Wrap It Up (Conclusion)*

While the conclusion may seem like it's not important and just an insignificant part of the petition for review, it only seems that way.

The conclusion is where you want to be clear as to the exact relief you are requesting and why. Use the conclusion to sum up your arguments in one or two sentences and explain the type of relief you are requesting. Do not simply state that you want a new trial or to be resentenced, or whatever the relief is you are requesting. Be detailed.

For example, explain that you are entitled to a new sentence because your trial attorney failed to present the mitigation outlined in the pro per petition for post-conviction relief, including failing to get a neuropsychological evaluation done, failing to call witnesses at sentence and failing to present sufficient argument at sentencing.

The judge will appreciate knowing the exact relief you are requesting—it will help him or her evaluate your claim more efficiently. And if relief other than what you are requesting is available, the court of appeals will be sure to give you that option.

5. HOW LONG WILL THE PROCESS TAKE?

There is no set time for the Court of Appeals to decide a petition for review. **Rule 32.9(c)** does not limit the Court of Appeals to any sort of deadline. I've seen petitions for review decided in a matter of a few weeks and others take approximately one year.

After you file your petition for review, expect to wait several months for a decision. If it comes earlier, that's great. If it comes later, be patient. The court will eventually decide your case—hopefully in your favor. Filing a request for a ruling or any other pleading will not speed up the review of your case.

M. PETITION FOR FURTHER REVIEW (ARIZONA SUPREME COURT)

If the Court of Appeals does not decide your petition for review in your favor, then you have two options. The first is to file a Petition for Further Review with the Arizona Supreme Court. The Petition for Further Review is formatted and written the same way as the Petition for Review to the Court of Appeals.

For a Petition for Further Review to be considered by the Arizona Supreme Court, your issue must be of statewide importance. Almost all Petitions for Further Review are denied, especially when the Court of Appeals issues an unpublished memorandum decision versus a published opinion.

You file the Petition for Further Review by mailing the original plus five copies to the Arizona Supreme Court at the following address:

Arizona Supreme Court
Attn: Clerk of the Court
1501 W. Washington, Suite 402
Phoenix, Ariz. 85007

Phone: (602)452-3396
As with the Petition for Review with the Court of Appeals, there is no set time for the Arizona Supreme Court to Rule on your petition—it could be a couple of months or a year.

N. GOING TO FEDERAL COURT

The second option, if your petition for review to the Court of Appeals is denied, is to proceed to federal court.

CRITICAL TIP: In order to have a federal issue to raise in federal court, you must have written your petition for post-conviction relief and petition for review with the federal issue clearly argued. There are several procedural default rules that will be used against you if you have not exhausted your federal claims in state court prior to bringing your case to federal court.

An entire manual could be written on *how to draft and file* a Petition for Writ of Habeas Corpus in federal court. This is not that manual. Instead, the prison is supposed to supply you with the forms and instructions necessary to prepare and file your federal petition for writ of habeas corpus. The instructions and forms can also be found on the District of Arizona Court's website: azd.uscourt.gov/forms.

For purposes of this manual, you'll need to know *how to federalize your Rule 32 petition* and avoid federal procedural defaults. Ordinarily, a federal court may not grant a petition for writ of habeas corpus unless the petition has exhausted available state remedies. 28 U.S.C. § 2254(b). To exhaust state remedies, a petitioner must afford the state courts the opportunity to rule upon the merits of his federal claims by "fairly presenting" them to the state's "highest" court in a procedurally appropriate manner. *Baldwin v. Reese*, 541 U.S. 27, 29 (2004)("to provide the State with the necessary 'opportunity,' the prisoner must 'fairly present' his claim in each appropriate state court…thereby alerting that court to the federal nature of the claim"); *Castille v. Peoples*, 489 U.S. 346, 349 (1989).

A claim has been fairly presented if you have described both the operative facts and the federal legal theory on which your claim is based. *Baldwin v. Reese*, 541 U.S. 27, 33 (2004). A "state prisoner does not 'fairly present' a claim to a state court if that court must read beyond the petition or brief…that does not alert it to the presence of a federal claim in order to find material, such as a lower court opinion in the case, that does so." *Baldwin*, 541 U.S. at 31-32. That means you have to present your claims (federal) at the very beginning of your case (the superior court for Rule 32 purposes), in your petition for post-conviction relief "by providing the proper factual and legal basis for the claim." *Insyxiengmay v. Morgan*, 403 F.3d 657, 668 (9th Cir. 2005). In other words, you have to give the State court a fair chance to properly decide your federal issues before asking the federal court to decide those issues.

Your claims may be precluded if you failed to properly present the claims in State court and returning your case to State court to do so would be "futile" because of the State court's procedural rules—such as waiver or preclusion in filing a successive Rule 32 petition—would bar the State court from considering the previously unraised claims. *Teague v. Lane*, 489 U.S. 288, 297-299 (1989).

Your federal claim may also be procedurally barred if, despite properly raising the federal claim in State court, the State court found the claim barred on State procedural grounds. *Beard v. Kindler*, 558 U.S. 53 (2009). So your federal claims will be barred if the State court relied "on a state-law ground that is both 'independent' of the merits of the federal claim and an 'adequate' basis for the court's decision." *Harris v. Reed*, 489 U.S. 255, 260 (1989).

A state procedural ruling is "independent" if the application of the bar does not depend on an antecedent ruling on the merits of the federal claim. And it is "adequate" if it is "strictly or regularly followed." *Wells v. Maass*, 28 F.3d 1005, 1010 (9th Cir. 1994).

Despite all of these procedural default rules which are designed to bar your federal claims, federal courts retain the power to consider the merits of procedurally defaulted claims. *Reed v. Ross*, 468 U.S. 1, 9 (1984). Typically, a federal court will not review the merits of a procedurally defaulted claim unless you demonstrate "cause" for the failure to properly exhaust the claim in State court and "prejudice" from the alleged constitutional violation, or you show that a "fundamental miscarriage of justice" would result if the claim were not heard on the merits. *Coleman v. Thompson*, 501 U.S. 722, 750 (1991). But be careful, because the federal court also holds the power to dismiss plainly meritless claims regardless of whether the claim was properly exhausted in State court. *Rhines v. Weber*, 544 U.S. 269, 277 (2005).

Therefore, you should mix the federal and state analysis together so there is a better chance that the State court will not parse out the state-law grounds to decide your issue. Or, you can cite to and analyze predominantly federal law and only make antidotal cites to State law so the court will be obligated to analyze the federal law.

APPENDIX A

<u>Arizona Rules of Criminal Procedure, Rule 32.1, et seq.</u>

RULE 32. OTHER POST-CONVICTION RELIEF

Rule 32.1. Scope of remedy

Subject to the limitations of Rule 32.2, any person who has been convicted of, or sentenced for, a criminal offense may, without payment of any fee, institute a proceeding to secure appropriate relief.

Any person who pled guilty or no contest, admitted a probation violation, or whose probation was automatically violated based upon a plea of guilty or no contest shall have the right to file a post-conviction relief proceeding, and this proceeding shall be known as a Rule 32 of-right proceeding.

Grounds for relief are:

a. The conviction or the sentence was in violation of the Constitution of the United States or of the State of Arizona;

b. The court was without jurisdiction to render judgment or to impose sentence;

c. The sentence imposed exceeded the maximum authorized by law, or is otherwise not in accordance with the sentence authorized by law;

d. The person is being held in custody after the sentence imposed has expired;

e. Newly discovered material facts probably exist and such facts probably would have changed the verdict or sentence. Newly discovered material facts exist if:

(1) The newly discovered material facts were discovered after the trial.

(2) The defendant exercised due diligence in securing the newly discovered material facts.

(3) The newly discovered material facts are not merely cumulative or used solely for impeachment, unless the impeachment evidence substantially undermines testimony which was of critical significance at trial such that the evidence probably would have changed the verdict or sentence.

f. The defendant's failure to file a notice of post-conviction relief of-right or notice of appeal within the prescribed time was without fault on the defendant's part; or

g. There has been a significant change in the law that if determined to apply to defendant's case would probably overturn the defendant's conviction or sentence; or

h. The defendant demonstrates by clear and convincing evidence that the facts underlying the claim would be sufficient to establish that no reasonable fact-finder would have found defendant guilty of the underlying offense beyond a reasonable doubt, or that the court would not have imposed the death penalty.

Rule 32.2. Preclusion of remedy

a. Preclusion. A defendant shall be precluded from relief under this rule based upon any ground:

(1) Raisable on direct appeal under Rule 31 or on post-trial motion under Rule 24;

(2) Finally adjudicated on the merits on appeal or in any previous collateral proceeding;

(3) That has been waived at trial, on appeal, or in any previous collateral proceeding.

b. Exceptions. Rule 32.2(a) shall not apply to claims for relief based on Rules 32.1(d), (e), (f), (g) and (h). When a claim under Rules 32.1(d), (e), (f), (g) and (h) is to be raised in a successive or untimely post-conviction relief proceeding, the notice of post-conviction relief must set forth the substance of the specific exception and the reasons for not raising the claim in the previous petition or in a timely manner. If the specific exception and meritorious reasons do not appear substantiating the claim and indicating why the claim was not stated in the previous petition or in a timely manner, the notice shall be summarily dismissed.

c. Standard of proof. The state shall plead and prove any ground of preclusion by a preponderance of the evidence. Though the state has the burden to plead and prove grounds of preclusion, any court on review of the record may determine and hold that an issue is precluded regardless of whether the state raises preclusion.

Rule 32.3. Nature of proceeding and relation to other remedies

This proceeding is part of the original criminal action and not a separate action. It displaces and incorporates all trial court post-trial remedies except post-trial motions and habeas corpus. If a defendant applies for a writ of habeas corpus in a trial court having jurisdiction of his or her person raising any claim attacking the validity of his or her conviction or sentence, that court shall under this rule transfer the cause to the court where the defendant was convicted or sentenced and the latter court shall treat it as a petition for relief under this rule and the procedures of this rule shall govern.

Rule 32.4. Commencement of proceedings

a. Form, Filing and Service of Petition. A proceeding is commenced by timely filing a notice of post-conviction relief with the court in which the conviction occurred. The court shall provide notice forms for commencement of all post-conviction relief proceedings. In a Rule 32 of-right proceeding, the notice must be filed within ninety days after the entry of judgment and sentence or within thirty days after the issuance of the final order or mandate by the appellate court in the petitioner's first petition for post-conviction relief proceeding. In all other non-capital cases, the notice must be filed within ninety days after the entry of judgment and sentence or within thirty days after the issuance of the order and mandate in the direct appeal, whichever is the later. In a capital case, the clerk of the Supreme Court shall expeditiously file a notice for post-conviction relief with the trial court upon the issuance of a mandate affirming the defendant's conviction and sentence on direct appeal. Any notice not timely filed may only raise claims pursuant to Rule 32.1(d), (e), (f), (g) or (h). The notice shall bear the caption of the original criminal action or actions to which it pertains. On receipt of the notice, the court shall file a copy of the notice in the case file of each such original action and promptly send copies to the defendant, the county attorney, the defendant's attorney, if known, and the attorney general or the prosecutor, noting in the record the date and manner of sending the copies. If the conviction occurred in a court other than the Superior Court, the copy shall be sent to the office of the prosecuting attorney who represented the state at trial. The state shall notify any victim who has requested notice of post-conviction proceedings.

b. Notification of Appellate Court. If an appeal of the defendant's conviction, sentence, or both is pending, the clerk, or the court, within 5 days after the filing of the notice for post-conviction relief, shall send a copy of the notice to the appropriate appellate court, noting in the record the date and manner of sending the copies.

c. Appointment of Counsel.

(1) Capital Cases. After the Supreme Court has affirmed a defendant's conviction and sentence in a capital case, the Supreme Court, or if authorized by the Supreme Court, the presiding judge of the county from which the case originated, shall appoint counsel for the defendant pursuant to A.R.S. § 13-4041 and Rule 6.8 if the defendant is determined to be indigent. If the appointment is made by the presiding judge, a copy of the court's order appointing counsel shall be filed in the Supreme Court.

Upon the filing of a successive notice, the presiding judge shall appoint the previous post-conviction counsel of the capital defendant unless counsel is waived or good cause is shown to appoint another qualified attorney from the list described in A.R.S. § 13-4041.

On the first notice in capital cases, appointed counsel for the defendant shall have one hundred twenty days from the filing of the notice to file a petition raising claims under Rule 32.1. A capital defendant proceeding without counsel shall have one hundred twenty days from the filing of the notice to file a petition. On the filing of a successive notice, appointed counsel, or the defendant if proceeding without counsel, shall file the petition within thirty days from the filing of the notice. On a showing of good cause, a defendant in a capital case may be granted a sixty day extension in which to file the petition. Additional extensions of thirty days may be granted for good cause. If a petition for post-conviction relief is not filed within one hundred and eighty days from the date of appointment of counsel, or one hundred and eighty days from the date the notice is filed, or the date a request for counsel is denied if the defendant is proceeding without counsel, the defendant or counsel for the defendant shall file a notice in the Supreme Court, advising the court of the status of the proceedings. Thereafter, defendant or counsel for the defendant shall file status reports in the Supreme Court every sixty days until the petition for post-conviction relief is filed.

(2) Rule 32 of-right and non-capital cases. Upon the filing of a timely or first notice in a Rule 32 proceeding, the presiding judge, or his or her designee, shall appoint counsel for the defendant within 15 days if requested and the defendant is determined to be indigent. Upon the filing of all other notices in non-capital cases, the appointment of counsel is within the discretion of the presiding judge. In non-capital cases appointed counsel for the defendant shall have sixty days from the date of appointment to file a petition raising claims under Rule 32.1. On a showing of good cause, a defendant in a non-capital case may be granted a thirty day extension within which to file the petition. Additional extensions of thirty days shall be granted only upon a showing of extraordinary circumstances.

In a Rule 32 of-right proceeding, counsel shall investigate the defendant's case for any and all colorable claims. If counsel determines there are no colorable claims which can be raised on the defendant's behalf, counsel shall file a notice advising the court of this determination. Counsel's role is then limited to acting as advisory counsel until the trial court's final determination. Upon receipt of the notice, the court shall extend the time for filing a petition by the defendant in propria persona. The extension shall be 45 days from the date the notice is filed. Any extensions beyond the 45 days shall be granted only upon a showing of extraordinary circumstances.

A defendant proceeding without counsel shall have sixty days to file a petition from the date the notice is filed or from the date the request for counsel is denied.

d. Transcript Preparation. If the trial court proceedings have not been previously transcribed, the defendant may request on a form provided by the clerk of court that certified transcripts be prepared. The court shall expeditiously review the request and order only those transcripts prepared that it deems necessary to resolve the issues to be raised in the petition. The preparation of the transcripts shall be at county expense if the defendant is indigent. The time for filing the petition shall be tolled from the time a request for the transcripts is made until the transcripts are prepared or the request is denied. Certified transcripts shall be prepared and filed within sixty days of the order granting the request.

e. Assignment of Judge. The proceeding shall be assigned to the sentencing judge where possible. If it appears that the sentencing judge's testimony will be relevant, that judge shall transfer the case to another judge.

f. Stay of Execution of Death Sentence; Notification by Supreme Court. If the defendant has received a sentence of death and the Supreme Court has fixed the time for execution of the sentence, no stay of execution shall be granted upon the filing of a successive petition except upon separate application for a stay to the Supreme Court, setting forth with particularity those issues not precluded under Rule 32.2. The Clerk of the Supreme Court shall notify the defendant, the Attorney General, and the Director of the State Department of Corrections of the granting of a stay.

Rule 32.5. Contents of petition

The defendant shall include every ground known to him or her for vacating, reducing, correcting or otherwise changing all judgments or sentences imposed upon him or her, and certify that he or she has done so. Facts within the defendant's personal knowledge shall be noted separately from other allegations of fact and shall be under oath. Affidavits, records, or other evidence currently available to the defendant supporting the allegations of the petition shall be attached to it. Legal and record citations and memoranda of points and authorities are required. In Rule 32 of-right and non-capital cases, the petition shall not exceed 25 pages. The response shall not exceed 25 pages, and any reply shall not exceed 10 pages. In capital cases, the petition shall not exceed 40 pages. The response shall not exceed 40 pages, and any reply shall not exceed 20 pages. A petition which fails to comply with this rule shall be returned by the court to the defendant for revision with an order specifying how the petition fails to comply with the rule. A petition that has been revised to comply with the rule shall be returned by the defendant for re-filing within 30 days after defendant's receipt of the non-complying petition. If the petition is not so returned, the court shall dismiss the proceedings with prejudice. The period for response by the state shall begin on the date a returned petition is re-filed.

Rule 32.6. Additional pleadings; summary disposition; amendments

a. Prosecutor's Response. Forty-five days after the filing of the petition, the state shall file with the court and send to the defendant or counsel for the defendant, a response. Affidavits, records or other evidence available to the state contradicting the allegations of the petition shall be attached to it. On a showing of good cause, the state may be granted a thirty-day extension to file a response. Additional extensions shall be granted only upon a showing of extraordinary circumstances.

b. Defendant's Reply. Within fifteen days after receipt of the response, the defendant may file a reply. Extensions shall be granted only upon a showing of extraordinary circumstances.

c. Summary Disposition. The court shall review the petition within twenty days after the defendant's reply was due. On reviewing the petition, response, reply, files and records, and disregarding defects of form, the court shall identify all claims that are procedurally precluded under this rule. If the court, after identifying all precluded claims, determines that no remaining claim presents a material issue of fact or law which would entitle the defendant to relief under this rule and that no purpose would be served by any further proceedings, the court shall order the petition dismissed. If the court does not dismiss the petition, the court shall set a hearing within thirty days on those claims that present a material issue of fact or law. If a hearing is ordered, the state shall notify the victims, upon the victims' request pursuant to statute or court rule relating to victims' rights, of the time and place of the hearing.

d. Amendment of Pleadings. After the filing of a post-conviction relief petition, no amendments shall be permitted except by leave of court upon a showing of good cause.

Rule 32.7. Informal conference

The court may at any time hold an informal conference to expedite the proceeding. The defendant need not be present if the defendant is represented by counsel who is present.

Rule 32.8. Evidentiary hearing

a. Evidentiary Hearing. The defendant shall be entitled to a hearing to determine issues of material fact, with the right to be present and to subpoena witnesses. If facilities are available, the court may, in its discretion, order the hearing to be held at the place where the defendant is confined, giving at least 15 days notice to the officer in charge of the confinement facility. In superior court, the hearing shall be recorded.
b. Evidence. The rules of evidence applicable in criminal proceedings shall apply, except that the defendant may be called to testify at the hearing.
c. Burden of Proof. The defendant shall have the burden of proving the allegations of fact by a preponderance of the evidence. If a constitutional defect is proven, the state shall have the burden of proving that the defect was harmless beyond a reasonable doubt.
d. Decision. The court shall rule within 10 days after the hearing ends except in extraordinary circumstances where the volume of the evidence or the complexity of the issues require additional time. If the court finds in favor of the defendant, it shall enter an appropriate order with respect to the conviction, sentence or detention, any further proceedings, including a new trial and conditions of release, and other matters that may be necessary and proper. The court shall make specific findings of fact, and state expressly its conclusions of law relating to each issue presented.
e. Transcript. The court may, and shall upon request of a party within the time for filing a petition for review, order that a certified transcript of the evidentiary hearing be prepared. The preparation of the evidentiary hearing transcript shall be at county expense if the defendant is indigent.

Rule 32.9. Review

a. Motion for Rehearing; Response; Reply. Any party aggrieved by a final decision of the trial court in these proceedings may, within fifteen days after the ruling of the court, move the court for a rehearing setting forth in detail the grounds wherein it is believed the court erred. No response to a motion for rehearing will be filed unless requested by the court, but a motion for rehearing will not be granted in the absence of such a response. A reply, if any, shall be filed within 10 days after the service of the response. The filing of a motion for rehearing in the trial court is not a prerequisite to the filing of a petition for review pursuant to paragraph (c) of this rule.
b. Disposition When Motion Granted. If the motion for rehearing is granted, the court may either (1) amend its previous ruling without a hearing, or (2) grant a new hearing and then either amend or reaffirm its previous ruling. In either case, if the court amends its previous ruling, it shall set forth its reasons for amending the previous ruling. The state shall notify the victim, upon request, of any action taken by the court.
c. Petition for Review. Within thirty days after the final decision of the trial court on the petition for post-conviction relief or the motion for rehearing, any party aggrieved may petition the appropriate appellate court for review of the actions of the trial court. A cross-petition for review may be filed within 15 days after service of a petition for review. The petition for review, cross-petition and all responsive pleadings filed pursuant to this rule shall be filed in the appellate court. Within 3 days after filing a petition or cross-petition for review, the petitioner and cross-petitioner, if any, shall file a notice of such filing with the trial court. The notice of filing may include a designation of record adding to the record defined in Rule 32.9(e) any additional certified transcripts of trial court proceedings that were prepared pursuant to Rule 32.4(d) or that were otherwise available to the trial court and the parties and that are material to the issues raised in the petition for review. Motions for extensions of time to file petitions or cross-petitions shall be filed in and ruled upon by the trial court. All other motions shall be filed in the court in which the petition is to be filed.
1. Form and contents. The petition or cross-petition for review shall comply with the form requirements of Rule 31.12 of the rules of criminal appellate procedure and contain a caption setting forth the name of the appellate court, the title of the case, a space for the appellate court case number, the trial court case number and a brief descriptive title. An original and seven copies of the petition and an original and one copy of the appendix, if any, shall be filed if review is being sought in the Supreme Court. An original and four copies of the petition and an original and one copy of the appendix, if any, shall be filed if review is being sought in the Court of Appeals. An original and one copy shall be filed if review is being sought in the superior court. The parties shall be designated as in the trial court proceedings. The petition or cross-petition shall not exceed 20 pages, exclusive of the appendix, shall not have a cover or be bound, but shall be fastened with a single staple in the upper left corner, and shall contain the following:
(i) Copies of the trial court's rulings entered pursuant to rules 32.6(c), 32.8(d) and 32.9(b).
(ii) The issues which were decided by the trial court and which the defendant wishes to present to the appellate court for review.
(iii) The facts material to a consideration of the issues presented for review.
(iv) The reasons why the petition should be granted. In capital cases all references to the record in the trial court shall be supported by an appendix, with appropriate copies of the portions of the record which support the petition. The petition shall not incorporate any document by reference, except the appendices. If the appendices

exclusive of the trial court's rulings exceed 15 pages in length, such appendices shall be fastened together separately from the petition and the copies of the trial court's rulings.

In Rule 32 of-right and non-capital cases, an appendix is not required, but the petition for review shall contain specific references to the record.

The filing of a motion for rehearing pursuant to paragraph (a) of this rule does not limit the issues that may be raised in the petition or the cross-petition for review. Failure to raise any issue that could be raised in the petition or the cross-petition for review shall constitute waiver of appellate review of that issue.

2. Service; Response; Reply. The petitioner or cross-petitioner shall serve a copy of the petition or cross-petition on the adverse party. A response may be filed within 30 days from the date upon which the petition or cross-petition is served. The response shall comply with the form requirements of Rule 32.9(c)(1) and shall not exceed 20 pages, exclusive of any appendix. Appendices shall conform to the requirements of Rule 32.9(c)(1). A reply, if any, may be filed within 10 days after the service of a response. The reply shall also comply with the form requirements of Rule 32.9(c)(1). The reply shall be limited to matters addressed in the response and shall not exceed 10 pages. No appendices shall be submitted with a reply.

d. Stay Pending Review. A motion for rehearing or a petition for review filed by the state pursuant to this section shall stay an order granting a new trial until final review is completed. For any other relief granted to a defendant, a stay pending further review is within the discretion of the trial or appellate court. The state shall notify the victim upon request of any action taken.

e. Filing of the Record. In Rule 32 of-right and non-capital cases, within 45 days after the receipt of the notice of filing of a petition for review, the record, including the trial court file and the certified transcript, shall be transmitted to the appellate court.

In capital cases, the record of the post-conviction proceedings shall not be transmitted to the appellate court unless requested by that court. If requested by the appellate court, the record shall consist of copies of the notice of post-conviction relief, the petition for post-conviction relief, response and reply, all motions and responsive pleadings filed and all minute entries and orders issued in the post- conviction proceedings, plus the certified transcript and any exhibits admitted by the trial court in the post-conviction proceedings.

f. Disposition When Petition Granted. The appellate court may, in its discretion, grant review and may order oral argument upon the petition if deemed necessary and may issue such orders and grant such relief as it deems necessary and proper. The state shall notify the victim, upon request, of any action taken by the appellate court.

g. Reconsideration and Review of Appellate Court Decision. The provisions governing the filing of motions for reconsideration and petitions for review in criminal appeals set forth in Rules 31.18 and 31.19 shall apply to and govern motions for reconsideration and petitions for review of an appellate court decision entered pursuant to Rule 32.

h. Return of the Record. In Rule 32 of-right-and non-capital cases, when the matter is determined, the clerk of the appellate court shall return the record to the appropriate trial court for retention according to law. In capital cases, the clerk of the appellate court shall return any exhibits to the appropriate trial court.

Rule 32.10. Extensions of time; notification of victims

In any capital case, if the victim has filed a notice of appearance as specified in A.R.S. § 13-4234.01, a party seeking an extension of time to file a brief must provide notice of the request to the victim. Notice shall be provided through the prosecutor's office handling the post-conviction relief proceeding, unless the victim specifies a different method in the notice of appearance. The victim may specify in the notice of appearance whether notification should be served directly on the victim or on another person, including the prosecutor, and whether service may be made electronically, by telephone, or by regular mail. If the victim has requested direct notification, the party seeking an extension of time shall serve notice on the victim within 24 hours of filing the extension request. If the prosecutor has the duty to notify the victim on behalf of the defendant, the prosecutor shall serve notice within 24 hours of receipt of the extension request. Service shall be made in the manner specified in the notice of appearance, or if no method is specified, by regular mail. In ruling on any request for an extension of a time limit set in this rule, the court shall consider the rights of the defendant and any victim to prompt and final conclusion of the case.

The following case law synopses are provided as a part of this manual. The synopses are a brief statement as to what the cases hold and their application to Rule 32. For a better understanding of the case and how it relates to your particular case, you should read the full case and any other cases relating to the case. **These case synopses are provided as guidance only and should not be solely relied upon to support your legal arguments.**

OPERATION & COMPLIANCE WITH RULE 32.1

Petitioners who plead guilty are entitled to file a petition for post-conviction relief under Rule 32, called an "of-right proceeding." A petition for post-conviction relief is a form of "direct review," and thus, federal habeas statute of limitations did not begin to run until 90 days after the Arizona Supreme Court denied petition for review. State court must have full and fair opportunity to decide all federal issues. *Summers v. Schriro*, 481 F.3d 710 (2007).

An actual innocence claim under Rule 32 is not typically subject to preclusion rule. In addition, when a defendant challenges the sufficiency of the evidence on direct appeal, he is not precluded from raising an actual innocence claim under Rule 32. The actual innocence claim still requires a defendant to demonstrate by clear and convincing evidence that the facts underlying the claim would be sufficient to establish that no reasonable fact-finder would have found him guilty of the underlying offense beyond a reasonable doubt. *State v. Denz*, 232 Ariz. 441, 306 P.3d 98 (App. Div.2 2013).

Blakely v. Washington requires a jury to determine any fact other than prior convictions that increases sentence beyond the statutory maximum. Blakely applies to cases pending on direct review or on review of a trial court's denial of a pleading defendant's "of right" petition for post-conviction relief. *State v. Cleere*, 210 Ariz. 212, 109 P.3d 107 (App. Div.2 2005), review granted, opinion vacated on remand 213 Ariz. 54, 138 P.3d 1181.

Petitions for post-conviction relief are controlled by the Arizona Rules of Procedure and are not to be considered a second appeal for the same issues. *Canion v. Cole ex rel. County of Maricopa*, 208 Ariz. 133, 91 P.3d 355 (App. Div.1 2004).

A notice of post-conviction relief (as well as the petition) is to be filed following sentencing and not following the guilty verdict. The triggering event is the pronouncement of sentence, not the finding of guilt. *State v. Saenz*, 197 Ariz. 487, 4 P.3d 1030 (App. Div.2 2000).

The rules of procedure governing petitions for post-conviction relief must be meticulously followed or petitioners will have been deemed to waive the right to file a petition for post-conviction relief. *State v. Carriger*, 143 Ariz. 142, 692 P.2d 991 (1984), certiorari denied 105 S.Ct. 2347, 471 U.S. 1111, 85 L.Ed.2d 864.

REMEDIES/PROCEDURAL BARS

Failure to raise a claim in Rule 32 proceedings will be procedurally barred in federal habeas corpus proceedings. *Van Norman v. Schriro*, 616 F.Supp.2d 939 (D.Ariz.2007), affirmed 362 Fed.Appx. 597, certiorari denied 130 S.Ct. 2355, 559 U.S. 1054, 176 L.Ed.2d 570.

Failure of the State to contest DNA test results in post-conviction relief proceedings constitutes waiver and a defendant may file a petition for post-conviction relief in accordance with the post-conviction rule, which then governs the proceedings, including any right to an evidentiary hearing. *State v. Gutierrez*, 229 Ariz. 573, 278 P.3d 1276 (2012).

Trial courts are not required to conduct *Anders*-type review for fundamental error whenever defendant exercises right to file pro per petition for post-conviction relief after appointed counsel refuses to proceed, but rather may summarily dismiss petition if appropriate. *Montgomery v. Sheldon*, 181 Ariz. 256, 889 P.2d 614 (1995), supplemented 182 Ariz. 118, 893 P.2d 1281.

The trial court should grant the request for an evidentiary hearing when petitioner presents a colorable claim (a claim that, if true, might have changed outcome of the proceedings. *State v. Runningeagle*, 176 Ariz. 59, 859 P.2d 169 (1993), certiorari denied 114 S.Ct. 609, 510 U.S. 1015, 126 L.Ed.2d 574 motion to recall mandate denied.

Issues decided on direct appeal cannot be properly raised in a petition for post-conviction relief. *State v. Wallace*, 160 Ariz. 424, 773 P.2d 983 (1989), certiorari denied 110 S.Ct. 1513, 494 U.S. 1047, 108 L.Ed.2d 649, rehearing denied 110 S.Ct. 2607, 496 U.S. 913, 110 L.Ed.2d 286.

FORM OF REMEDY AVAILABLE

The right to file a petition for post-conviction relief is not a constitutional right but a right given to defendants by rule and may be revoked. *State v. Glassel*, 233 Ariz. 353, 312 P.3d 1119 (2013).

Although a "Rule 32 of-right" proceeding is a post-conviction relief proceeding, it is the functional equivalent of a direct appeal for a pleading defendant. *State v. Ward*, 211 Ariz. 158, 118 P.3d 1122 (App. Div.1 2005), review denied.

Rule 32 is available to defendants convicted of misdemeanor and felony offenses. *State v. Aguilar*, 170 Ariz. 292, 823 P.2d 1300 (App. Div.1 1991), review denied.

Rule 32 is designed to provide a remedy for constitutional errors involving a defendant's trial or direct appeal.   *State v. Krum*, 183 Ariz. 288, 903 P.2d 596 (1995).

An appeal is designed to give prompt, full appellate review to those who have grounds to believe they have not had a fair trial while Rules of Criminal Procedure, Rule 32.1 et seq. pertaining to post-conviction relief is designed to accommodate the unusual situation where justice ran its course and yet went awry, and such rule is a safeguard in addition to the many others that are part of our system, but it may not be abused. *State v. Carriger*, 143 Ariz. 142, 692 P.2d 991 (1984), certiorari denied 105 S.Ct. 2347, 471 U.S. 1111, 85 L.Ed.2d 864.

Exhaustion Requirements/Avoiding Federal Procedural Default

Exhaustion-of-remedies requirement does not prevent a state prisoner from petitioning for federal habeas relief from providing further facts to support claim in federal district court, as long as those facts do not fundamentally alter legal claim already considered by state courts. *Lopez v. Schriro*, 491 F.3d 1029 (D.Ariz.2007), certiorari denied 128 S.Ct. 1227, 552 U.S. 1224, 170 L.Ed.2d 140.

Unexhausted state claims would be treated as technically exhausted where habeas petitioner's previous failures to satisfy exhaustion requirement had resulted in nearly nine years of delay, and were petitioner to return to state court, state court would determine that he had procedurally defaulted. *Lambright v. Lewis*, 932 F.Supp. 1547 (D.Ariz.1996), reversed 167 F.3d 477, rehearing granted, opinion withdrawn 177 F.3d 901, on rehearing 191 F.3d 1181, on remand 220 F.3d 1022, affirmed in part, reversed in part 241 F.3d 1201.

Successive Petitions

The rules precluding successive claims raised in petitions for post-conviction relief that had been waived, or that had been or could have been raised on direct appeal, exist to prevent multiple petitions for post-conviction, not to avoid post-conviction review entirely. *State v. Petty*, 225 Ariz. 369, 238 P.3d 637 (App. Div.2 2010).

Trial Court's Discretion

The appellate court will not disturb a trial court's order denying petition for post-conviction relief unless the court clearly has abused its discretion. *State v. Denz*, 232 Ariz. 441, 306 P.3d 98 (App. Div.2 2013).

Petitions for post-conviction relief are addressed to sound discretion of the trial court, and decision of trial court will not be reversed unless abuse of discretion affirmatively appears. *State v. Wilson*, 179 Ariz. 17, 875 P.2d 1322 (App. Div.1 1993), review denied.

Fundamental Error Review

A defendant will only have fundamental error review available when trial attorney fails to object to potential error in a case. *State v. Gendron*, 168 Ariz. 153, 812 P.2d 626 (1991).

Fundamental error is that which is "clear, egregious and curable only via a new trial." *State v. Gendron*, 168 Ariz. 153, 812 P.2d 626 (1991).

To prevail under this standard of review, a defendant must establish both that fundamental error exists and that the error in his case caused him prejudice. *State v. Gendron*, 168 Ariz. 153, 812 P.2d 626 (1991).

Fundamental error occurs when the defendant loses a right essential to his defense, was unable to receive a fair trial, or where the error goes to the very foundation of the defendant's theory of the case. *State v. Valenzuela*, 194 Ariz. 404, 984 P.2d 12 (1999).

HYBRID REPRESENTATION – DISCRETION

No hybrid representation, allowable only within trial court's discretion in limited circumstances, or improper alternating representation occurred from defendants' pro se filing of petitions for post-conviction relief after appointed counsel refused to proceed, despite fact that counsel failed to formally withdraw; appointed counsel never presented case for defendants. *Montgomery v. Sheldon*, 181 Ariz. 256, 889 P.2d 614 (1995), supplemented 182 Ariz. 118, 893 P.2d 1281.

PROBATION VIOLATION

Rule 32 allows a defendant, under certain circumstances, to attack factual or legal basis for admission of probation violation or to attack process by which admission of probation violation was accepted by the judge. *Wilson v. Ellis*, 176 Ariz. 121, 859 P.2d 744 (1993).

WHAT CONSTITUTES A COLORABLE CLAIM – EVIDENTIARY HEARING

The proper inquiry regarding a court granting an evidentiary hearing concerns whether, "if appellant's contentions are taken as true, do they successfully show ineffective assistance of counsel?" *State v. Suarez*, 23 Ariz.App. 45, 530 P.2d 402 (1975).

The Arizona Supreme Court has held that a petitioner is invariably entitled to an evidentiary hearing where a colorable claim – one that, "if the defendant's allegations are true, might have changed the outcome" – is presented. *State v. Spreitz*, 202 Ariz. 1, 39 P.3d 525 (2002)(en banc), citing *State v. Watton*, 164 Ariz. at 328, 793 P.2d at 85, citing *State v. Schrock*, 149 Ariz. 433, 441, 719 P.2d 1049, 1057 (1986).

"A petitioner need not provide detailed evidence, but must provide specific factual allegations that, if true, would entitle him to relief." *United States v. Hearst*, 638 F.2d 1190, 1194 (9th Cir. 1980).

The Court must assume all of Petitioner's claims in a petition for post-conviction relief to be true, and make its determination as to whether a hearing is warranted based strictly upon that assumption. *State v. Fillmore*, 187 Ariz. 174, 927 P.2d 1303 (1996).

Third-party affidavits showing no personal knowledge are, at most, hearsay evidence rather than direct evidence of recantation, and standing alone such affidavits will seldom entitle petitioner to post-conviction relief. *State v. Krum*, 183 Ariz. 288, 903 P.2d 596 (1995).

However meritorious or non-meritorious a post-conviction claim may be, it cannot be addressed until petitioner has had adequate opportunity to present it to the court. *Montgomery v. Superior Court In and For County of Maricopa*, 178 Ariz. 84, 870 P.2d 1180

(App. Div.1 1993), review granted, affirmed as modified 181 Ariz. 256, 889 P.2d 614, supplemented 182 Ariz. 118, 893 P.2d 1281.

Trial court did not abuse its discretion in denying a defendant's petition for post-conviction relief, which was based on alleged failure to disclose *Brady* material and allegation of juror misconduct, where petition did not present a "colorable claim." *State v. Adamson*, 136 Ariz. 250, 665 P.2d 972 (1983), certiorari denied 104 S.Ct. 204, 464 U.S. 865, 78 L.Ed.2d 178.

Defendant was not entitled to a post-conviction evidentiary hearing concerning claim that he did not have an opportunity to review presentence report and correct incorrect material contained in presentence report, because no evidence was presented which would indicate that he was not afforded an opportunity to read his presentence report, because he made no colorable claim that the statements alleged to be incorrect in the presentence report were in fact untrue, and because he did not show how he had been prejudiced by the failure to read the probation report. *State v. Gunter*, 132 Ariz. 64, 643 P.2d 1034 (App. Div.1 1982).

INEFFECTIVE ASSISTANCE OF COUNSEL

To prove ineffective assistance of counsel, a petitioner must show that counsel's representation fell below the standard of care in the profession and that the petitioner was prejudiced. *Strickland v. Washington*, 466 U.S. 668 (1984)

Both prongs of the *Strickland* test must be satisfied. *State v. Walton*, 159 Ariz. 571, 769 P.2d 1017 (1989); U.S. Const. Amends. 5, 6 & 14; Ariz. Const., Art. 2 §§ 4 &24.

Whether or not to call a witness to testify can support a claim of ineffective assistance of counsel claim. *Morris v. State of Cal.*, 966 F.2d 448 (Cal. 1991).

Court of appeals was not at liberty to disregard precedent of state supreme court and create right for non-pleading defendants to effective representation in post-conviction proceedings due to limited nature of federal habeas review. *State v. Escareno-Meraz*, 232 Ariz. 586, 307 P.3d 1013 (App. Div.2 2013), review denied, certiorari denied 134 S.Ct. 1943, 188 L.Ed.2d 967.

Decision of the United States Supreme Court in *Martinez v. Ryan*, determining that defendants had "equitable" right to effective assistance of initial post-conviction counsel, did not constitute significant change in state law entitling post-conviction petitioner to raise claim of ineffective assistance of post-conviction counsel, where Supreme Court did not ground its decision in a constitutional right and limited its decision to application of procedural default in federal habeas review. *State v. Escareno-Meraz*, 232 Ariz. 586, 307 P.3d 1013 (App. Div.2 2013), review denied, certiorari denied 134 S.Ct. 1943, 188 L.Ed.2d 967.

Non-pleading defendants have no constitutional right to counsel in post-conviction proceedings; thus, despite the existence of state rules providing counsel, a claim that post-conviction counsel was ineffective is not a cognizable ground for relief in a subsequent post-conviction proceeding. *State v. Escareno-Meraz*, 232 Ariz. 586, 307 P.3d 1013 (App. Div.2 2013), review denied, certiorari denied 134 S.Ct. 1943, 188 L.Ed.2d 967.

The right to the effective assistance of counsel in the first post-conviction proceeding is meaningless unless the pleading, indigent defendant is afforded counsel in a second proceeding challenging the alleged ineffective assistance of counsel in the first proceeding, and it must be a different attorney than the one who represented the defendant in the first proceeding. *Osterkamp v. Browning*, 226 Ariz. 485, 250 P.3d 551 (App. Div.2 2011).

Ineffective assistance of counsel claims are to be brought in post-conviction relief proceedings, and any such claims inaccurately raised in a direct appeal will not be addressed by appellate courts regardless of merit. *State v. Sang Le*, 221 Ariz. 580, 212 P.3d 918 (App. Div.2 2009), review denied.

Defendant may bring ineffective assistance of counsel claims only in a post-conviction proceeding, and not before trial, at trial, or on appeal. *State ex rel. Thomas v. Rayes*, 214 Ariz. 411, 153 P.3d 1040 (2007).

A defendant may state a claim for post-conviction relief on the basis that counsel's ineffective assistance led the defendant to make an uninformed decision to reject a plea bargain and proceed to trial. *State v. Donald*, 198 Ariz. 406, 10 P.3d 1193 (App. Div.1 2000), review denied, certiorari denied 122 S.Ct. 63, 534 U.S. 825, 151 L.Ed.2d 30.

To establish deficient performance during plea negotiations, as element of ineffective assistance of counsel, a defendant must prove that the lawyer either: (1) gave erroneous advice, or (2) failed to give information necessary to allow defendant to make an informed decision whether to accept the plea. *State v. Donald*, 198 Ariz. 406, 10 P.3d 1193 (App. Div.1 2000), review denied, certiorari denied 122 S.Ct. 63, 534 U.S. 825, 151 L.Ed.2d 30.

To establish prejudice in the defendant's rejection of a plea offer, as element of claim of ineffective assistance of counsel, a defendant must show a reasonable probability that, absent his attorney's deficient advice, he would have accepted the plea offer and declined to go forward to trial. *State v. Donald*, 198 Ariz. 406, 10 P.3d 1193 (App. Div.1 2000), review denied, certiorari denied 122 S.Ct. 63, 534 U.S. 825, 151 L.Ed.2d 30.

A defendant may inferentially show prejudice from defendant's rejection of plea agreement, as element of ineffective assistance of counsel, by establishing a serious negative consequence, such as receipt of a substantially longer or harsher sentence than would have been imposed as a result of a plea. *State v. Donald*, 198 Ariz. 406, 10 P.3d 1193 (App. Div.1 2000), review denied, certiorari denied 122 S.Ct. 63, 534 U.S. 825, 151 L.Ed.2d 30.

Defendant may show prejudice from defendant's rejection of plea agreement, as element of ineffective assistance of counsel, by showing that the risks inherent in proceeding to trial so substantially outweighed the benefits of the plea that proceeding to trial was an unreasonable risk. *State v. Donald*, 198 Ariz. 406, 10 P.3d 1193 (App. Div.1 2000), review denied, certiorari denied 122 S.Ct. 63, 534 U.S. 825, 151 L.Ed.2d 30.

A defendant is not required to prove that the trial court would have accepted the plea agreement in order to establish prejudice resulting from counsel's deficient advice, which caused defendant to reject a plea bargain. *State v. Donald*, 198 Ariz. 406, 10 P.3d 1193 (App. Div.1 2000), review denied, certiorari denied 122 S.Ct. 63, 534 U.S. 825, 151 L.Ed.2d 30.

State and defendant are free to negotiate a different plea agreement, if a new trial is ordered as remedy for ineffective assistance of counsel regarding defendant's rejection of original plea offer, but any plea agreement, including the one originally offered, must be subject to the approval and acceptance of the court. *State v. Donald*, 198 Ariz. 406, 10 P.3d 1193 (App. Div.1 2000), review denied, certiorari denied 122 S.Ct. 63, 534 U.S. 825, 151 L.Ed.2d 30.

If the passage of time, the erosion of evidence, or the disappearance of witnesses has impaired the State's ability to retry the case, it would be unfair to order a new trial as the remedy for ineffective assistance of counsel which caused defendant to reject original plea offer, and in such a case, the defendant's acceptance of the original plea offer might be the sole avenue of relief. *State v. Donald*, 198 Ariz. 406, 10 P.3d 1193 (App. Div.1 2000), review denied, certiorari denied 122 S.Ct. 63, 534 U.S. 825, 151 L.Ed.2d 30.

Claim that trial counsel made tactical decisions violating defendant's right to the effective assistance of counsel should be pursued by a petition for post-conviction relief rather than on direct appeal. *State v. Mach*, 198 Ariz. 183, 8 P.3d 371 (App. Div.2 2000), review denied and opinion ordered not published 199 Ariz. 472, 19 P.3d 613.

Claims of ineffective assistance of counsel are properly raised under rule pertaining to post-conviction relief rather than on direct appeal. *State v. Geotis*, 187 Ariz. 521, 930 P.2d 1324 (App. Div.1 1996), review denied 189 Ariz. 109, 938 P.2d 1110.

A pleading defendant must be afforded an opportunity to assert a claim regarding effectiveness of attorney representing him on first petition for post-conviction relief, the equivalent of a challenged representation of counsel on direct appeal, and the obvious method is by means of the second petition for post-conviction relief. *State v. Pruett*, 185 Ariz. 128, 912 P.2d 1357 (App. Div.1 1995), review denied.

PRO PER REPRESENTATION

Defendant's constitutional right to appellate review may be exercised through pro per petition for post-conviction relief if appointed counsel declines to provide assistance; defendant is not required to decide at commencement of post-conviction proceeding whether to proceed pro per or to request counsel. *Montgomery v. Sheldon*, 181 Ariz. 256, 889 P.2d 614 (1995), supplemented 182 Ariz. 118, 893 P.2d 1281.

If court determines post-conviction issue may have merit, court provides assistance of counsel to argue issue prior to making its decision; allowing appointed counsel to remain of record pending filing of post-conviction motion pro per facilitates this process. *Montgomery v. Superior Court In and For County of Maricopa*, 178 Ariz. 84, 870 P.2d 1180 (App. Div.1 1993), review granted, affirmed as modified 181 Ariz. 256, 889 P.2d 614, supplemented 182 Ariz. 118, 893 P.2d 1281.

Rationale for allowing post-conviction petitioner to proceed pro per after counsel determines that there is no viable basis for post-conviction petition is to provide review of what petitioner personally believes to be his or her basis for relief. *Montgomery v. Superior Court In and For County of Maricopa*, 178 Ariz. 84, 870 P.2d 1180 (App. Div.1 1993), review granted, affirmed as modified 181 Ariz. 256, 889 P.2d 614, supplemented 182 Ariz. 118, 893 P.2d 1281.

Defendant was entitled to present his claims pro se in post-conviction proceeding following appointed counsel's notification to defendant that counsel could not find meritorious issue. *Montgomery v. Superior Court In and For County of Maricopa*, 178 Ariz. 84, 870 P.2d 1180 (App. Div.1 1993), review granted, affirmed as modified 181 Ariz. 256, 889 P.2d 614, supplemented 182 Ariz. 118, 893 P.2d 1281.

PLEADING DEFENDANTS

For defendants who plead guilty, a proceeding for post-conviction relief is the only means available for exercising the constitutional right to appellate review. *State v. Ward*, 211 Ariz. 158, 118 P.3d 1122 (App. Div.1 2005), review denied.

Prejudice in the context of a guilty plea is satisfied when post-conviction petitioner demonstrates a reasonable probability that, but for counsel's errors, he would not have pleaded guilty and would have insisted on going to trial. *State v. Bowers*, 192 Ariz. 419, 966 P.2d 1023 (App. Div.1 1998), review denied.

To state a colorable claim of ineffective assistance of counsel in post-conviction proceeding in which petitioner seeks to withdraw his guilty plea, the allegation that petitioner would not have pleaded guilty but for counsel's deficient performance must be accompanied by an allegation of specific facts which would allow a court to meaningfully assess why that deficiency was material to the plea decision. *State v. Bowers*, 192 Ariz. 419, 966 P.2d 1023 (App. Div.1 1998), review denied.

Allegations of post-conviction petitioner who pled guilty to two counts of armed robbery, that he was misled by counsel's erroneous advice that convictions would effectively result in a minimum term of 50 years imprisonment because the sentences had to be served consecutively to each other, stated colorable claim of ineffective assistance of counsel. *State v. Bowers*, 192 Ariz. 419, 966 P.2d 1023 (App. Div.1 1998), review denied.

Allegations of post-conviction petitioner who pled guilty to two counts of armed robbery, that counsel misled him by informing him that convictions after a trial would result in sentences that would have to be served consecutively to sentences for offenses for which petitioner was on probation, stated colorable claim of ineffective assistance of counsel, although plea agreement contained no provision regarding the other sentences. *State v. Bowers*, 192 Ariz. 419, 966 P.2d 1023 (App. Div.1 1998), review denied.
Post-conviction petitioner's allegation that counsel failed to advise him, at time he pled guilty to two counts of armed robbery, that conviction of armed robbery with a simulated weapon, a non-dangerous offense, would have exposed him to a maximum prison sentence of 15.75 years on each offense, failed to state colorable claim of ineffective assistance of counsel, absent allegation that petitioner's plea decision would have changed in reliance upon possible conviction of non-dangerous offenses. *State v. Bowers*, 192 Ariz. 419, 966 P.2d 1023 (App. Div.1 1998), review denied.

Guilty plea cannot waive the right to all appellate review, as state constitution requires that some form of appeal be available even when defendant pleads guilty; however, defendant pleading guilty does waive any direct appeal, and thus, only appellate review for defendant pleading guilty is by the much narrower avenue under rule providing for other post-conviction relief. *Montgomery v. Sheldon*, 181 Ariz. 256, 889 P.2d 614 (1995), supplemented 182 Ariz. 118, 893 P.2d 1281.

Because post-conviction relief, under rule for relief other than by direct appeal or post-trial motion, is the only appeal for defendant pleading guilty, statute requires court of appeals to search for fundamental error in post-conviction record while considering petition for review of denial of post-conviction relief. *Montgomery v. Sheldon*, 181 Ariz. 256, 889 P.2d 614 (1995), supplemented 182 Ariz. 118, 893 P.2d 1281.

Review of denial of post-conviction relief is discretionary, even though post-conviction record must be reviewed for fundamental error when defendant pled guilty; court of appeals is not required to grant defendant's petition for review before searching record for fundamental error, or to perfunctorily grant review and deny relief to search for fundamental error, nor must it file memorandum decision; written decision or opinion is required only if court finds fundamental error, thus Court of Appeals may still summarily reject claims in petition, and deny review by summary order, simply stating in any order denying review that it has examined the record and found no fundamental error. *Montgomery v. Sheldon*, 181 Ariz. 256, 889 P.2d 614 (1995), supplemented 182 Ariz. 118, 893 P.2d 1281.

IMPRISONMENT AFTER SENTENCE EXPIRATION

Issue whether the Department of Corrections improperly forfeited 240 days of good time credit earned by the petitioner was subject to being considered by the Supreme Court on State's petition for review in post-conviction matter, even though issue was mooted by petitioner's release, where issue was of statewide importance, affecting many prisoners, and was capable of repetition, yet evaded review. *State v. Valenzuela*, 144 Ariz. 43, 695 P.2d 732 (1985).

CLAIM OF NEWLY DISCOVERED EVIDENCE

Motions for a new trial based on newly discovered evidence are disfavored and should be granted with great caution. *State v. Hess*, 231 Ariz. 80, 290 P.3d 473 (App. Div.2 2012).

For post-conviction relief to be granted on the basis of newly discovered evidence, the evidence must have been in existence at the time of trial, but not discovered until after trial. *State v. Sanchez*, 200 Ariz. 163, 24 P.3d 610 (App. Div.2 2001).

Motion for new trial based on newly discovered evidence, brought 38 days after guilty verdict was rendered but prior to sentencing, was premature under rules governing petitions for post-conviction relief and motions to vacate judgment and was untimely under rule governing motions for new trial based on the verdict. *State v. Saenz*, 197 Ariz. 487, 4 P.3d 1030 (App. Div.2 2000), review denied.

Evidence known to defendant during trial is not newly discovered, for purposes of motion for new trial, even if it is not known to his counsel. *State v. Saenz*, 197 Ariz. 487, 4 P.3d 1030 (App. Div.2 2000), review denied.

To be considered newly discovered, in the context of motion for new trial, evidence must truly be newly discovered, i.e., discovered after trial. *State v. Saenz*, 197 Ariz. 487, 4 P.3d 1030 (App. Div.2 2000), review denied.

"In order to be entitled to post-conviction relief on the ground of newly discovered evidence under Rule 32.1(e), a defendant must establish that the evidence was discovered after trial although it existed before trial [and] that it could not have been discovered and produced at trial through reasonable diligence...." *State v. Saenz*, 197 Ariz. 487, ¶7, 4 P.3d 1030, 1032 (App.2000).

To justify post-conviction relief on basis of newly discovered evidence, evidence must have existed at time of trial, but have been discovered after trial; evidence must not be simply cumulative or impeaching; evidence must be relevant; and evidence must be such that it would likely have altered verdict, finding or sentence if known at time of trial. *State v. Pac*, 175 Ariz. 189, 854 P.2d 1175 (App. Div.1 1993), review denied.

Colorable claim in newly discovered evidence case, which requires evidentiary hearing on motion for post-conviction relief, is present if: evidence appears on its face to have existed at time of trial but was discovered after trial; motion alleges facts from which court could conclude that defendant was diligent in discovering facts and bringing them to court's attention; evidence is not simply cumulative or impeaching; evidence is relevant to case; and evidence is such that it would likely have altered verdict, finding, or sentence if known at time of trial. *State v. Bilke*, 162 Ariz. 51, 781 P.2d 28 (1989).

COURT'S DISCRETION REGARDING NEWLY DISCOVERED EVIDENCE

Denying murder defendant's motion to vacate judgment on ground of newly discovered evidence was not an abuse of discretion; proffered witness was not credible and witness' testimony was not newly discovered evidence. *State v. Dunlap*, 187 Ariz. 441, 930 P.2d 518 (App. Div.1 1996), review denied, certiorari denied 117 S.Ct. 2456, 520 U.S. 1275, 138 L.Ed.2d 214.

In first-degree murder prosecution, trial court did not abuse its discretion in denying defendant's motion for new trial based on newly discovered evidence consisting of store operator's testimony that she saw victims in her store near 11:00 on night of murder and testimony of two members of desert party, which took place in vicinity of murder scene on night of murder, that they heard no gunshots in time span between 7:30 and 11:30, leaving inference that murders were committed at later time, in that none of such testimony, if heard by jury, would have affected verdict given state's production of evidence contradicting such testimony. *State v. Macumber*, 119 Ariz. 516, 582 P.2d 162 (1978), certiorari denied 99 S.Ct. 621, 439 U.S. 1006, 58 L.Ed.2d 683.

Trial court did not abuse its discretion in drug prosecution in refusing to grant new trial on basis of newly discovered evidence, where it was improbable that new evidence would have changed verdict and there was no apparent reason why defendant could not have secured that testimony for trial. *State v. Mann*, 117 Ariz. 517, 573 P.2d 917 (App. Div.1 1977).

Defendant failed to raise even colorable claim for post-conviction relief based on newly discovered evidence of third party's prior sexual molestation of defendant's daughter, though such evidence would allegedly have undercut medical evidence presented by state that daughter's hymen was broken as tending to suggest that defendant had molested her, in light of defendant's admissions to police officers and other overwhelming evidence of defendant's guilt. *State v. Boldrey*, 176 Ariz. 378, 861 P.2d 663 (App. Div.2 1993), review denied.

"Discovery" by a different defense attorney after trial that defendant's photograph was the only photograph in a photographic lineup depicting a person in blue denim did not constitute a "newly-discovered material fact" within scope of this rule; the fact was not "newly discovered," but was merely a fact that was not argued at pretrial suppression hearing by defendant's trial counsel. *State v. Dogan*, 150 Ariz. 595, 724 P.2d 1264 (App. Div.2 1986).

Evidence that petitioner's photograph analysis expert conducted a computer-enhanced analysis of several photographic trial exhibits and concluded that the photographic evidence produced by the state before petitioner's trial for murder, kidnapping, robbery, and theft was altered and that some photographs had been omitted and not produced to petitioner during discovery was not sufficient to establish that no reasonable fact-finder would have found petitioner guilty of the underlying offense beyond a reasonable doubt, so as to permit petitioner to bring a post-conviction due process claim under Brady based on that evidence under exception to Arizona rule precluding post-conviction relief (PCR) on any claim that could have been raised on direct appeal or in a prior PCR petition, particularly given the ample evidence of petitioner's guilty that existed beyond the footprint and photographic evidence. *Henry v. Ryan*, 720 F.3d 1073 (D.Ariz.2013), rehearing denied, certiorari denied 134 S.Ct. 2729.

DNA test results submitted by post-conviction petitioner in support of his petition for relief based on newly discovered evidence were unlikely to affect verdict; petitioner submitted test results excluding him as donor of sperm found in victim's vagina and on toilet seat, state's evidence established that defendant did not ejaculate during his sexual assault of victim, that neither he nor victim touched toilet during kidnapping and assault, and that sperm found in victim's vagina was that of her husband-to-be resulting from their recent sexual intercourse, evidence of defendant's guilt was strong, and state did not rely on presence of semen in victim's vagina at trial.   *State v. Hess*, 231 Ariz. 80, 290 P.3d 473 (App. Div.2 2012).

Defendant's claim that crime laboratory's change in blood-testing procedure after defendant's driving while under the influence (DUI) trial was admission of faulty procedure, did not present a colorable claim of newly discovered evidence in post-conviction relief proceeding and would not have altered trial court's denial of defendant's motion to suppress blood test results, where there were no allegations of laboratory error, and change in procedure did not occur until after trial. *State v. Sanchez*, 200 Ariz. 163, 24 P.3d 610 (App. Div.2 2001).

Prisoner's post-trial diagnosis, that he was suffering from posttraumatic stress disorder at time of offenses as result of his combat military service in Vietnam, constituted colorable claim of newly discovered evidence that might have affected prisoner's sentence, and thus prisoner was entitled to evidentiary hearing on his post-conviction relief motion. *State v. Bilke*, 162 Ariz. 51, 781 P.2d 28 (1989).

Newly discovered evidence, which at best related version of evidence which inculpated defendant's wife but did nothing to exculpate defendant, convicted of murdering his two daughters by setting fire to their bedroom, did not warrant new trial, since it could not be said that newly discovered evidence, if introduced at new trial, would probably change verdict. *State v. Knapp*, 127 Ariz. 65, 618 P.2d 235 (1980).

NEWLY DISCOVERED EVIDENCE – PETITIONER'S DUE DILIGENCE

Any post-trial facts regarding statements by co-defendant's former cellmate that may have been exculpatory to capital defendant with respect to his death sentence for his conviction on two counts of first-degree murder were not newly discovered, as required by Arizona's criminal procedure rule providing grounds for post-conviction relief if newly discovered material facts probably existed and would have changed verdict or sentence, thus precluding capital defendant's Brady claim, regardless of correctness of Arizona rule's materiality standard for Brady claim, where capital defendant could have exercised minimal diligence to secure interview or testimony from co-defendant's cellmate to determine whether his statements were exculpatory and material. *Runningeagle v. Ryan*, 686 F.3d 758 (D.Ariz.2012), certiorari denied 133 S.Ct. 2766, 186 L.Ed.2d 233.

Habeas petitioner's claim that execution by lethal injection violated the Eighth Amendment was procedurally defaulted, given that petitioner did not exercise due diligence in obtaining evidence, in the form of statements of doctors, that indicated death by lethal injection likely caused suffering and torture. *Williams v. Stewart*, 441 F.3d 1030 (D.Ariz.2006), certiorari denied 127 S.Ct. 510, 549 U.S. 1002, 166 L.Ed.2d 381.

Post-conviction petitioner's lack of diligence in requesting DNA testing warranted denial of his petition, where form of DNA testing sought was available 10 years before petitioner brought petition which led to claim of newly discovered evidence. *State v. Hess*, 231 Ariz. 80, 290 P.3d 473 (App. Div.2 2012).

Defendant seeking relief on a claim of newly discovered evidence must demonstrate that he or she exercised due diligence in securing the newly discovered material facts; that is, the defendant must show he or she was diligent in pursuing a remedy. *State v. Hess*, 231 Ariz. 80, 290 P.3d 473 (App. Div.2 2012).

Trial court did not abuse its discretion during post-conviction relief proceedings in determining that jury note to trial judge during deliberations and trial judge's response to that note did not constitute newly discovered evidence; trial court's findings of fact and legal conclusions suggested it determined the note and the trial judge's response had existed at the time of trial and, through the exercise of diligence, could have been discovered previously. *State v. Swoopes*, 216 Ariz. 390, 166 P.3d 945 (App. Div.2 2007), review denied.

Evidence is not "newly discovered," for purposes of motion for new trial, unless it was unknown to the trial court, the defendant, or counsel at the time of trial and neither the defendant nor counsel could have known about its existence by the exercise of due diligence. *State v. Saenz*, 197 Ariz. 487, 4 P.3d 1030 (App. Div.2 2000), review denied.

NEWLY DISCOVERED EVIDENCE REGARDING WITNESSES

Where a defendant knows of the existence and identity of a witness before trial and makes no effort to obtain the witness' testimony, such testimony will not ordinarily justify a new trial. *State v. Saenz*, 197 Ariz. 487, 4 P.3d 1030 (App. Div.2 2000), review denied.

Affidavit of witness was not newly discovered evidence to support claim for post-conviction relief, where parties knew that witness was at defendant's house at time of shooting and counsel interviewed him before trial. *State v. Andersen*, 177 Ariz. 381, 868 P.2d 964 (App. Div.1 1993), review denied, certiorari denied 114 S.Ct. 2717, 512 U.S. 1224, 129 L.Ed.2d 842.

Credibility of recanted evidence is controlling factor best determined by trial judge in post-conviction relief proceeding, as courts have long been skeptical of recanted testimony claims, even when professed by accuser in court. *State v. Krum*, 183 Ariz. 288, 903 P.2d 596 (1995).
Affidavits submitted by defendant in post-conviction relief proceeding, alleging that victim recanted his trial testimony by stating that his father never molested him and that undue influence was brought to bear on seven-year-old victim by his maternal grandmother, presented colorable claim so as to entitle defendant to evidentiary hearing on recantation issue. *State v. Wagstaff*, 161 Ariz. 66, 775 P.2d 1130 (App. Div.1 1988), approved as modified 164 Ariz. 485, 794 P.2d 118.

Although recanted testimony is not favored as being "inherently unreliable," trial judge is in best position to evaluate its credibility and effect for purposes of motion to vacate judgment on basis of newly discovered evidence. *State v. Hickle*, 133 Ariz. 234, 650 P.2d 1216 (1982).

CHALLENGES TO PRISON SENTENCE

Blakely v. Washington, under which any fact other than prior conviction used to increase sentence beyond statutory maximum must be found by jury, applies to cases pending on review of a trial court's denial of a pleading defendant's "of-right" petition for post-conviction relief. *State v. Cleere*, 213 Ariz. 54, 138 P.3d 1181 (App. Div.2 2006), review denied.

Defendant's second petition for post-conviction relief was "of right," such that *Blakely v. Washington*, under which any fact other than prior conviction used to increase sentence beyond statutory maximum must be found by jury, applied, because it followed a conviction pursuant to a plea agreement and trial court's resentencing. *State v. Cleere*, 213 Ariz. 54, 138 P.3d 1181 (App. Div.2 2006), review denied.

Blakely v. Washington, which requires that any fact other than prior conviction used to increase sentence beyond statutory maximum be found by jury, applied to petitioner's "Rule 32 of-right" proceeding that was still pending when *Blakely* was decided. *State v. Ward*, 211 Ariz. 158, 118 P.3d 1122 (App. Div.1 2005), review denied.
Rule permitting post-conviction relief when the sentence imposed is "not in accordance with the sentence authorized by law" encompasses a claim that a sentence was not imposed in compliance with the relevant sentencing law, at least for a sentence imposed on a

defendant who was convicted pursuant to a guilty plea. *State v. Cazares*, 205 Ariz. 425, 72 P.3d 355 (App. Div.2 2003), review denied.

Defendant failed to make even threshold showing of gross disproportionality in consecutive 12, 19, 19 and 22-year sentences imposed for his repeated abuse of position of trust in sexually abusing his 11-year-old daughter, and was not even entitled to evidentiary hearing on his petition for post-conviction relief. *State v. Boldrey*, 176 Ariz. 378, 861 P.2d 663 (App. Div.2 1993), review denied.

Petition for post-conviction relief is correct procedure for defendant to seek remedy for court's failure to advise defendant, who admitted to violation of probation in revocation hearing, that admission could be used against him at trial on criminal charges. *State v. Glad*, 170 Ariz. 483, 826 P.2d 346 (App. Div.1 1992).

A defendant wishing to challenge a prior conviction used to enhance a sentence when that issue was not raised in trial court was to submit matter to trial court by petition for post-conviction relief, rather than challenge conviction by appeal. *State v. Anderson*, 160 Ariz. 412, 773 P.2d 971 (1989).

Sentences imposed upon defendant convicted of robbery and murder in the first degree must be set aside where the attorney's conduct at sentencing stage approached that of a neutral observer. *State v. Carriger*, 132 Ariz. 301, 645 P.2d 816 (1982).

Petitioner's general allegation that sentencing judges considered prior standards for parole eligibility in determining sentences for lewd and lascivious charges and for drug charge was insufficient to show a colorable claim for relief; moreover, it did not appear that sentencing judges considered parole eligibility in imposition of either of his sentences. *State v. Walden*, 126 Ariz. 333, 615 P.2d 11 (App. Div.1 1980).

WHAT CONSTITUTES A VALID SENTENCE

The appellate court will find an abuse of sentencing discretion only if the trial court acted arbitrarily or capriciously or failed to adequately investigate the facts relevant to sentencing. *State v. Cazares*, 205 Ariz. 425, 72 P.3d 355 (App. Div.2 2003), review denied.

A trial court has broad discretion to determine the appropriate penalty to impose upon conviction, and the appellate court will not disturb a sentence that is within statutory limits unless it clearly appears that the court abused its discretion. *State v. Cazares*, 205 Ariz. 425, 72 P.3d 355 (App. Div.2 2003), review denied.

Court of Appeals would not intervene to reduce sentences imposed upon defendant convicted of kidnapping and attempt to commit rape where sentences were within the statutory limits and circumstances of kidnapping and attempted rape and of defendant's alcoholism justified sentencing court in concluding that the objectives of sentencing would best be served by severe penalty. *State v. Daniel*, 25 Ariz.App. 592, 545 P.2d 440 (App. Div.2 1976).

MODIFICATION OF PRISON SENTENCE

Petitioner met burden of proving by preponderant evidence that he was infected with Acquired Immune Deficiency Syndrome (AIDS) virus when his sentence was handed down so as to require new sentencing hearing on issue whether his condition warranted shorter prison term; fact that medical witness could only testify in terms of possibility and not of probability was not dispositive of petitioner's claim. *State v. Ellevan*, 179 Ariz. 382, 880 P.2d 139 (App. Div.1 1994).

PROBATION/PAROLE REVOCATION CLAIMS

Where allegations are made, which, if proven, are indicative of deprivation of defendant's rights which are not matter of record in probation revocation hearing, relief from probation revocation may be obtained through post-conviction review. *State v. Robbins*, 166 Ariz. 531, 803 P.2d 942 (App. Div.1 1991).

DELAYED APPEAL CLAIMS

Defendant was not without fault for delay in filing his petition for post-conviction from underlying conviction by guilty plea to attempted possession of a narcotic drug for sale, and thus, petition was appropriately denied as untimely; defendant regretted having failed to challenge his conviction after he violated his probation and in turn faced mandatory deportation, which did not fall within a recognized excuse for belated post-conviction filing. *State v. Poblete*, 227 Ariz. 537, 260 P.3d 1102 (App. Div.2 2011), review denied, certiorari denied 133 S.Ct. 1453, 185 L.Ed.2d 360.

For purposes of determining the preclusive effect of a petition for post-conviction relief setting forth a request for a delayed appeal, such a request is not a substantive request for relief, but a procedural gateway to the appellate court; the trial court, in evaluating such a request, does not review the trial, conviction, or sentence, and at most may be called on to make limited factual findings about post-trial communication between counsel and defendant regarding an appeal. *State v. Rosales*, 205 Ariz. 86, 66 P.3d 1263 (App. Div.2 2003).

Where defendant's form notice incorrectly assigned court of appeals as designated appellate forum after voluntary manslaughter conviction, although statutes require direct appeal to the supreme court in actions involving crimes for which life imprisonment has been imposed, defendant's request for delayed appeal, after his conviction was affirmed by the court of appeals and subsequent petitions for rehearing and review were denied, was correctly granted under this rule which permits criminal defendant appropriate delayed post-conviction relief when defendant's failure to appeal within prescribed time was without fault on his part. *State v. Canedo*, 125 Ariz. 197, 608 P.2d 774 (1980).

Burden Of Proof

It is post-conviction petitioner's burden to assert grounds that bring him within the provisions of rule governing post-conviction relief. *State v. Wilson*, 179 Ariz. 17, 875 P.2d 1322 (App. Div.1 1993), review denied.

Significant Change In Law

A change in the law that excuses an untimely post-conviction filing requires some transformative event; a clear break from the past. *State v. Poblete*, 227 Ariz. 537, 260 P.3d 1102 (App. Div.2 2011), review denied, certiorari denied 133 S.Ct. 1453, 185 L.Ed.2d 360.

Prior misunderstanding by lawyers about whether attempted sexual conduct with minor under 12 was dangerous crime against children, for purpose of enhancing sentence, which misunderstanding was clarified by Court of Appeals in *State v. Gonzalez*, did not establish that Gonzalez was significant change in law, as grounds for obtaining post-conviction review of defendant's claim, not raised in his initial post-conviction petition, that sexual conduct with minor under 15 was not dangerous crime against children as applied to his case where victim was less than 12 years old. *State v. Shrum*, 220 Ariz. 115, 203 P.3d 1175 (2009).

An appellate opinion is not a change in the law, as ground for obtaining post-conviction review of a claim that was not raised on direct appeal or in a prior post-conviction proceeding, simply because it reverses a trial court judgment; such correction of trial court legal error is a routine occurrence in appellate review, and no different conclusion is compelled merely because trial courts other than the one whose judgment is on appeal had previously made the same error. *State v. Shrum*, 220 Ariz. 115, 203 P.3d 1175 (2009).

Court of Appeals' decision in *State v. Gonzalez* that attempted sexual conduct with minor under age of 12 was not dangerous crime against children, for purposes of enhancing sentence, was not significant change in law, as ground for obtaining post-conviction review of claim not raised in prior post-conviction petition that sentence for sexual conduct with minor under age 15 could not be enhanced as dangerous crime against children, as applied to case where victim was under age 12; *Gonzalez* did not overrule any prior appellate decision, or rest on changed interpretation of constitutional law, but merely was first court to interpret statute. *State v. Shrum*, 220 Ariz. 115, 203 P.3d 1175 (2009).
A statutory or constitutional amendment representing a definite break from prior law can be a significant change in the law, as grounds for obtaining post-conviction review of a claim that was not raised on direct appeal or in a prior post-conviction proceeding. *State v. Shrum*, 220 Ariz. 115, 203 P.3d 1175 (2009).

The archetype of "a significant change in the law" occurs, for the purposes of obtaining post-conviction review of a claim that was not raised on direct appeal or in a prior post-conviction proceeding, when an appellate court overrules previously binding case law. *State v. Shrum*, 220 Ariz. 115, 203 P.3d 1175 (2009).

United States Supreme Court's *Apprendi* decision, which held that other than the fact of a prior conviction, any fact that increases the penalty for a crime beyond the prescribed statutory maximum must be submitted to a jury, and proved beyond a reasonable doubt, constitutes a significant change in federal constitutional law, and thus the Court of Appeals was obligated to follow the federal retroactivity analysis in deciding whether to apply Apprendi to persons whose convictions have become final. *State v. Sepulveda*, 201 Ariz. 158, 32 P.3d 1085 (App. Div.2 2001), review denied.

A new rule will apply to final convictions on collateral review only if it falls within one of two exceptions: new rule making certain conduct exempt from the legislature's power to define criminal acts, or a watershed rule of criminal procedure that implicates the fundamental fairness of the trial. *State v. Sepulveda*, 201 Ariz. 158, 32 P.3d 1085 (App. Div.2 2001), review denied.

The "significant change in law" exception to preclusion of claims not raised in post-conviction petition applied even though first petition was filed after decision establishing significant change of law, where subsequent decision entitling petitioner to retroactive application of the changed law was filed after the first petition was denied. *State v. Bonnell*, 171 Ariz. 435, 831 P.2d 434 (App. Div.1 1992).

PETITION FOR POST-CONVICTION RELIEF REVIEW

Defendant's death while his petition for post-conviction relief was pending was not a proper basis for the trial court to dismiss his indictment and conviction, even though the petition for post-conviction relief was defendant's first opportunity to raise his ineffective assistance of counsel claim, since defendant's convictions were presumed to have been regularly obtained and valid after his direct appellate process was complete. *State v. Glassel*, 233 Ariz. 353, 312 P.3d 1119 (2013).

Whether the court must set aside a validly obtained and affirmed conviction if the defendant dies while a post-conviction relief proceeding is pending is a question of law reviewed de novo. *State v. Glassel*, 233 Ariz. 353, 312 P.3d 1119 (2013).

The procedural device for delayed appeals, which is available to defendants in some circumstances, is not available to the state because determinable and speedy finality is an important constitutional and public policy consideration in favor of defendants in criminal prosecutions. *State v. Limon*, 229 Ariz. 22, 270 P.3d 849 (App. Div.2 2011).

A non-pleading defendant is entitled to a direct appeal with the assistance of counsel and has the parallel right to challenge the effectiveness of appellate counsel in what will usually be his or her first post-conviction proceeding, but has no constitutional right to counsel or effective assistance in post-conviction proceedings; although the non-pleading defendant has the right to effective representation on appeal, he has no valid, substantive claim for ineffective assistance on a prior post-conviction relief petition. *Osterkamp v. Browning*, 226 Ariz. 485, 250 P.3d 551 (App. Div.2 2011).

Review of decisions in post-conviction proceedings are governed exclusively by the provisions of Rules of Criminal Procedure, Rule 32.1 et seq. *State v. White*, 27 Ariz.App. 213, 553 P.2d 246 (App. Div.1 1976).

WAIVER OF CLAIMS

Defendant who waived direct appeal of claims arising by entering negotiated guilty plea to theft by control or misrepresentation had right to effective assistance of counsel on of-right post-conviction review, and therefore, second notice for post-conviction relief that asserted claim of ineffective assistance of post-conviction counsel was not impermissible attempt to seek successive post-conviction relief. *State v. Petty*, 225 Ariz. 369, 238 P.3d 637 (App. Div.2 2010).

The right to petition for post-conviction relief cannot be waived merely by a plea or admission. *State v. Ward*, 211 Ariz. 158, 118 P.3d 1122 (App. Div.1 2005), review denied.

Notice of post-conviction relief was not subject to summary dismissal as successive, where earlier petition did not waive potential substantive claims for relief from conviction or sentence; earlier petition was request for leave to file belated appeal, and had no preclusive effect on substantive claims. *State v. Rosales*, 205 Ariz. 86, 66 P.3d 1263 (App. Div.2 2003).

FORM #1

NAME: _____
ADDRESS:_____

_____

_____

(ACTING PRO PER)

IN THE SUPERIOR COURT OF ARIZONA
IN AND FOR THE COUNTY OF _____

STATE OF ARIZONA,
    Plaintiff,

v.

_____,

    Defendant.

Case No.: _____

**NOTICE OF POST-CONVICTION
RELIEF; REQUEST FOR
APPOINTMENT OF COUNSEL**

Hon. _____

PERSONAL INFORMATION

Defendant's Name and prison number: _____

Defendant's Address: _____

Defendant's Phone Number (if released): _____

CASE INFORMATION

Defendant's Case Number: _____

Defendant's Convictions (crimes): _____

_____

Defendant's Prison Sentence: _____

Date of Sentence: _____

Manner of Conviction:
[ ] Plea Agreement
[ ] Probation Violation (by agreement)
[ ] Probation Violation (following a hearing)
[ ] Bench Trial
[ ] Jury Trial

Has the defendant had a direct appeal (following a trial): [ ] Yes [ ] No

Has the defendant previously filed a petition for post-conviction relief or had previous Rule 32 proceedings regarding this conviction: [ ] Yes [ ] No

ATTORNEY INFORMATION

Defendant's Superior Court (either trial or change of plea) attorney(s):

_____

Did a different attorney represented the defendant at sentencing: [ ] Yes [ ] No
If yes, name: _____

Appeal attorney: _____

First Rule 32 Attorney (if any): _____

Is an ineffective assistance of counsel claim anticipated: [ ] Yes [ ] No

Is the defendant currently represented by an attorney for the Rule 32 proceedings before this Court: [ ] Yes [ ] No
If no, is the defendant requesting the appointment of counsel: [ ] Yes [ ] No

If this notice is untimely or is the second or later notice being filed with the Court in this case, do any of the following apply to defendant's potential Rule 32 claim(s):

[ ] Rule 32.1(d): The defendant is being held in custody after the sentence imposed has expired.

[ ] Rule 32.1(e): Newly discovered material facts exist which probably would have changed the verdict or sentence.

[ ] Rule 32.1(f): The defendant's failure to file a timely notice of post-conviction relief or notice of appeal was without fault on the defendant's part.

[ ] Rule 32.1(g): There has been a significant change in the law that would probably overturn the defendant's conviction or sentence.

[ ] Rule 32.1(h): Facts exist which establish by clear and convincing evidence that the defendant is actually innocent.

Briefly explain the reasons for failing to raise the above-selected claim in the previous petition for post-conviction relief:

_____

_____

I am requesting post-conviction relief. I understand that I must include in my petition every ground of relief known to me and which has not been raised and decided previously. I also understand that failure to raise any known ground for relief in my petition will prohibit me from raising it at any future date.

_____
Defendant's Signature

DATED: _____

AFFIDAVIT OF INDIGENCY
I have requested the appointment of a lawyer to represent me in post-conviction proceedings. I swear under oath and penalty of perjury that I am indigent and because of my poverty I am financially unable to pay for the cost of a lawyer to represent me without incurring substantial hardship to myself or my family.

I do solemnly swear and attest that the foregoing is accurate and true to the best of my knowledge.

DATED: _____

_____
Defendant's Signature

Sworn to before me and subscribed in my presence this ___ day of _____, 20___.

_____
Notary
My commission expires:_____

FORM #2

NAME: _____

ADDRESS:_____

_____

_____

(ACTING PRO PER)

IN THE SUPERIOR COURT OF ARIZONA
IN AND FOR THE COUNTY OF _____

STATE OF ARIZONA,

      Plaintiff,

v.

_____,

      Defendant.

Case No.: _____

SUBPOENA DUCES TECUM

Hon. _____

THE STATE OF ARIZONA TO:

Name: _____

Address: _____

_____

_____

Tel: _____

Fax: _____

THIS SUBPOENA ONLY APPLIES TO THE DUTIES CHECKED BELOW:

[ ]   **For Attendance of Witnesses at Hearing**
      YOU ARE COMMANDED to appear in the Superior Court of the State of Arizona, in and for the County of _____, at the place, date and time specified below, to testify at the Rule 32 Hearing:

Judicial Officer: _____

Courtroom: _____

Address: _____

Date: _____

Time: _____

Re: _____

[ ]   For Taking of Depostion

YOU ARE COMMANDED to appear at the place, date and time specified below to testify at the taking of a deposition in the above-captioned case.

Place of Deposition: _____

Address: _____

Date: _____

Time: _____

Method of Recording: _____

[ ]   For Production of Documentary Evidence or Inspection of Premises

YOU ARE COMMANDED to produce and permit inspection, copying, testing, and/or sampling of the following designated documents, electronically stored information or tangible things, or to permit the inspection of premises:

Documents or other listed materials:

_____

_____

_____

All above-referenced documents or other listed materials are to be produced as specified below:

Mailed to: _____

Address: _____

_____

By Date: _____

Time: _____

FORM #3

NAME: _____
ADDRESS:_____
_____
_____
(ACTING PRO PER)

IN THE SUPERIOR COURT OF ARIZONA
IN AND FOR THE COUNTY OF _____

STATE OF ARIZONA,	Case No.: _____
Plaintiff,	
v.	**ACCEPTANCE/WAIVER OF SERVICE OF PROCESS**
_____,	
Defendant.	Hon. _____

I, the undersigned party named below, swear under oath/affirm the following:

1. I have received a copy of the following documents on the ___ day of
    _____, 20__:

    Subpoena Duces Tecum issued on the ___ day of _____, 20__.

    I understand that my receipt of the above-referenced documents and my
signature below constitute

    [ ] the acceptance of service of process of these documents, OR

    [ ] a waiver of service of process and notice which may be prescribed by law.

DATED: _____   _____
                             Name:

FORM #4

NAME: _____

ADDRESS:_____

_____

_____

(ACTING PRO PER)

IN THE SUPERIOR COURT OF ARIZONA
IN AND FOR THE COUNTY OF _____

STATE OF ARIZONA,	Case No.: _____
Plaintiff,	
v.	**MOTION TO COMPEL DISCOVERY**
_____,	
Defendant.	Hon. _____

COMES NOW, the Defendant, _____, acting pro per, and respectfully requests that this Court compel disclosure from the following individuals and/or agencies:

_____

_____

_____

The undersigned defendant is requesting the following materials from the above named individuals and/or agencies:

_____

_____

_____

_____

The basis for this request is as follows:

A good faith effort has been made to obtain the above-referenced materials, to no avail. Undersigned defendant is aware, under *Canion v. Cole*, 210 Ariz. 598 (2005), that it is at this Court's discretion to order disclosure of the requested materials. Undersigned defendant is unable to properly prepared the pro per petition for post-conviction relief and/or reply to the State's Response to the Pro Per Petition for Post-Conviction Relief without obtaining the requested materials. As such, it is respectfully requested that this Court exercise its discretion and grant the motion to compel disclosure of the requested materials.

RESPECTFULLY SUBMITTED this ____ day of _____, 20__.

_____
Name:
Defendant, Acting Pro Per

FORM #5

THE HOPKINS LAW OFFICE, P.C.
10645 N. Oracle Rd., #121-326
Tucson, Arizona 85737
Telephone: 520.465.2658
Facsimile: 520.867.6509
objectionyourhonor@hotmail.com

Cedric Martin Hopkins, Esq.
California State Bar No. 226313
Arizona State Bar No. 22790

Attorney for

IN THE SUPERIOR COURT OF THE STATE OF ARIZONA

IN AND FOR THE COUNTY OF MARICOPA

STATE OF ARIZONA,	Case Number:
Plaintiff,	**PETITION FOR POST-CONVICTION RELIEF**
v.	
,	Hon. Bruce Cohen
Defendant.	Criminal Presiding

COMES NOW, Defendant, , by and through undersigned counsel, and hereby

submits her Petition for Post-Conviction Relief. Ariz.R.Crim.Proc., Rule 32.1. This

Petition is supported by the accompanying Memorandum of Points and Authorities.

RESPECTFULLY SUBMITTED this   day of   ,   .

THE HOPKINS LAW OFFICE, P.C.

/s/_____
Cedric Martin Hopkins, Esq.
Attorney for Petitioner

MEMORANDUM OF POINTS AND AUTHORITIES

I.

STATEMENT OF RELEVANT FACTS

The State charged Petitioner with one count of Armed Robbery and one count of Kidnapping, both class two dangerous felonies. ROA 1. Petitioner exercised her right to a jury trial with respect to the charges.

On March 14, 2008, a Wendy's restaurant in Tempe, Arizona was robbed. R.T., 10/19/10, p. 26:19 – p. 30:8. T.M., walked up to the drive-thru window and pointed a gun at the victim, R.D. Id. at p. 29:5-24. T.M. demanded money from R.D. and R.D. complied and gave T.M. approximately four hundred dollars. Id. at p. 30:6-18. After taking the money, T.M. turned and got into a vehicle that was parked behind him. Id at p. 31:1-4.

After the State called its witnesses, the defense rested without calling any witnesses. ROA 40. The jury then returned guilty verdicts for Armed Robbery and Kidnapping. Id. The jury found that both offenses were dangerous. Id. This Court sentenced Petitioner to a term of seven years in prison for each offense. ROA 47. The two prison terms were ordered to be served concurrent to one another. Id.

II.

STATEMENT OF PERTINENT FACTS WITHIN PETITIONER'S KNOWLEDGE

L.T. (defense counsel) represented Petitioner with respect to the trial and sentencing. Attachment A, Affidavit of Defendant. On several occasions, Petitioner requested that L.T. interview T.M.. Id. T.M. was the individual who robbed the Wendy's restaurant. Id. L.T. failed to interview T.M. or call T.M. to testify at

Petitioner's trial. Id. Had L.T. interviewed T.M., then L.T. would have discovered that Petitioner was not the driver of the vehicle in this case. Id. Therefore, T.M. would have testified that Petitioner was not the driver of the vehicle. Attachment B, Affidavit of T.M..

III.

ARGUMENT

A.   Defense counsel provided ineffective assistance of counsel in failing to call an eye-witness to the robbery.

To prove ineffective assistance of counsel, a petitioner must show that counsel's representation fell below the standard of care in the profession and that the petitioner was prejudiced. *Strickland v. Washington*, 466 U.S. 668 (1984)(both prongs of test must be satisfied); *State v. Walton*, 159 Ariz. 571, 769 P.2d 1017 (1989); U.S. Const. Amends. 5, 6 & 14; Ariz. Const., Art. 2 §§ 4 &24. Whether or not to call a witness to testify can support a claim of ineffective assistance of counsel claim. *Morris v. State of Cal.*, 966 F.2d 448 (Cal. 1991).

Deficient Performance

Petitioner was convicted solely upon R.D.'s testimony that he identified her as being the driver of the vehicle that participated in the robbery. R.D.'s testimony, however, shows that his identification of Petitioner was not credible.

R.D. testified that, "at one point...when the car drove behind T.M." he could see the driver of the vehicle. R.T., 10/19/10, p. 34:17-20. While the vehicle was stopped, R.D. admitted that he could not see the driver of the vehicle. Id. at p. 34:21-23. R.D. only got a look at the driver "for a couple of seconds," (R.T., 10/19/10, p.

59:12-16) while the car was in motion, "as it drove by the window." Id. at p. 34:24 – p. 35:1. R.D. also could not identify the driver's race.[1] Id. at p. 35:18-20. In fact, when asked if he gave a description of the driver when the police arrived at the Wendy's restaurant, R.D. said, "No. Not of the driver, no."[2] Id. at p. 40:20-22. R.D. admitted that when he signed his name on the photo line-up identifying Petitioner, he was not "sure if [the person in the photograph] was the person driving [the] car at all." Id. at p. 60:14-19. R.D. was unsure if he could identify the driver of the vehicle **because [he] didn't see that person.**" Id. at p. 68:25 – p. 69:3. And when R.D. circled Petitioner as the driver of the vehicle during the photo line-up, he testified **he was merely guessing.** Id. at p. 84:5-12. R.D. stated that even though he circled Petitioner picture, he **"cannot say that...[she] was the person that was driving that car."** Id.

Even during trial, R.D. did not identify Petitioner as the person who was the driver of the vehicle. Id. at p. 44:12-19. R.D. was asked directly: "Now, when do you see the black female [the driver of the vehicle]?" to which he replied, "I couldn't really see the black female." Id. at p. 67:15-16. On cross-examination, R.D.'s

_____

[1] The following exchange shows that R.D. was only able to identify the driver of the vehicle as a black female after being shown the photo line-up by the police:
    DEFENSE COUNSEL: "[R.D.], you said earlier that you didn't know the race of the person that drove the car.
    R.D.: "Correct."
    DEFENSE COUNSEL: "So then how can you tell the officer that it was a black female if you didn't know the person's race?"
    R.D.: "Because what – he had shown me the pictures, sir." R.T., 10/19/10, p. 70:3-9.

[2] R.D. stated that the description written down by the police officer regarding the driver was not the description he gave to the police. He was asked, "So when somebody puts in here, 'black female, thin build' as your description, that wasn't your description, was it?" R.D. responded, "No. Not that I remember today, no." R.T., 10/19/10, p. 68:21-24.

testimony unequivocally showed that he did not know if Petitioner was driving the vehicle:

DEFENSE COUNSEL: "[R.D.], as you sit there today, and as you go back in your memory to March 14th, isn't it fair to say you don't know if [Petitioner] was driving that car, do you?

R.D.: No. That's correct.

DEFENSE COUNSEL: So when people show you pictures and say, Oh, your memory is better today than it was in – you don't remember who the person was who drove the vehicle?

R.D.: Correct." R.T., 10/19/10, p. 71:4-12.

While R.D. could not recall identifying Petitioner, when asked if he could recall the license plate R.D. stated, "Oh, yes. Yes." Id. at p. 36:3-5. In fact, R.D.'s testimony clearly shows that he was focused solely on making sure he relayed the license plate number to police. R.D. stated, "[r]ight after the gentleman turned around to walk back into the car I grabbed the phone. I called the cops and I gave them exactly the license plate number." Id. at p. 36:6-9.
R.D.'s identification of Petitioner was unreliable. Defense counsel had an opportunity to rebut R.D.'s already weak testimony by calling the only other eye-witness to the incident, T.M.. Defense counsel chose not to call T.M. to testify at Petitioner's trial, however.

Not only did defense counsel not call T.M. to testify, defense counsel failed to even interview T.M.. Attachment B, Affidavit of T.M. Had defense counsel interviewed T.M., he would have discovered that T.M. would have testified that

Petitioner was not the driver of the vehicle. Attachment B. This evidence could have been presented to the jury. T.M.'s testimony, combined with R.D.'s inconsistent identification, would have resulted in Petitioner being found not guilty of the charges.

Defense counsel simply failed to ascertain whether T.M.'s testimony would have been helpful to Petitioner's defense. Attachemnt B. T.M. attempted to speak with defense counsel on several occasions, but defense counsel did not take T.M.'s statement. Id. As a result of not interviewing T.M. or calling him to testify to the facts noted above, defense counsel's performance was deficient as outlined in *Strickland.*

Prejudice to Petitioner

In Petitioner's case, identification was crucial. As shown above, R.D.'s identification of Petitioner was weak. Among other inconsistencies, R.D. resorted to guessing whether or not Petitioner was the actual driver of the vehicle. R.T., 10/19/10, p. 84:5-12. As such, it was paramount to have any other eyewitnesses to the robbery testify at trial.

In this case, the only other eye-witness to the robbery was T.M.. T.M.'s testimony would have been that Petitioner was not the driver of the vehicle. See, Attachment B. Had defense counsel called T.M. to testify, then the jury would have been able to consider evidence – that Petitioner was not the driver of the vehicle – which refuted R.D.'s skeletal identification of Petitioner. The jury would have had an entirely different view of this case – a view that would have supported Petitioner's innocence. It follows that Petitioner would have been found not guilty of the charges against her.

B.   Defense Counsel provided ineffective assistance of counsel in failing to file any motions on her behalf.

In this case, defense counsel did not challenge any of the evidence against Petitioner. Based upon the circumstances of the case along with R.D.'s trial testimony, it is clear that R.D.'s identification of Petitioner should have been challenged in a pre-trial motion. Defense counsel provided ineffective assistance of counsel in failing to challenge R.D.'s identification of Petitioner.

To prove ineffective assistance of counsel, a petitioner must show that counsel's representation fell below the standard of care in the profession and that the petitioner was prejudiced. *Strickland v. Washington*, 466 U.S. 668 (1984)(both prongs of test must be satisfied); *State v. Walton*, 159 Ariz. 571, 769 P.2d 1017 (1989); U.S. Const. Amends. 5, 6 & 14; Ariz. Const., Art. 2 §§ 4 &24.

As stated in *State v. Dessureault*, 104 Ariz. 380, 453 P.2d 951 (1969), "if at the trial the proposed in-court identification is challenged, the trial judge must immediately hold a hearing in the absence of the jury to determine from clear and convincing evidence whether it contained unduly suggestive circumstances." *Dessureault*, 104 Ariz. at 384, 453 P.2d at 955 (1969). The burden is on the State. Id. "It is the prosecution's burden to satisfy the trial judge from clear and convincing evidence that the proposed in-court identification is not tainted by the prior identification." Id. Had defense counsel requested, the trial court would have been obligated to "instruct the jury that before returning a verdict of guilty it must be satisfied beyond a reasonable doubt that the in-court identification was independent of the previous pretrial identification or if not derived from an independent source, it must find from other evidence in the case that the defendant is the guilty person beyond a reasonable doubt." Id.

In *Neil v. Biggers*, 409 U.S. 188 (1972), the United States Supreme Court outlined factors for the trial court to consider to ensure that an identification is reliable. *Biggers*, 409 U.S. at 199-200. The factors include: (1) the witness's opportunity to observe the suspect at the time of the crime; (2) the degree of attention of the witness; (3) the accuracy of a witness's prior description of the criminal; (4) the witness's level of certainty at the confrontation; and (5) the amount of time that passed between the crime and the confrontation. In examining each of the factors, R.D.'s identification of Petitioner was not reliable and should have been challenged by defense counsel.

a.   *R.D.'s opportunity to observe the criminal at the time of the crime.*

R.D. testified that, "at one point...when the car drove behind T.M." he could see the driver of the vehicle. R.T., 10/19/10, p. 34:17-20. While the vehicle was stopped, R.D. admitted that he could not see the driver of the vehicle. Id. at p. 34:21-23. R.D. only got a look at the driver "for a couple of seconds," (R.T., 10/19/10, p. 59:12-16) while the car was in motion, "as it drove by the window." Id. at p. 34:24 – p. 35:1. . R.D. was unsure if he could identify the driver of the vehicle "because [he] didn't see that person." Id. at p. 68:25 – p. 69:3.

With respect to the first factor, R.D. only saw the driver of the vehicle for two seconds. Therefore, R.D. did not have any meaningful opportunity to observe the criminal.

b.   *R.D.'s degree of attention.*

At trial, R.D. testified that his "number-one main concern is not somebody driving a car, but getting shot." R.T., 10/19/10, p. 59:17-21. R.D.'s other "main concern was just to give [T.M.] the money and make sure he didn't hurt none [sic] of my employees." R.T., 10/19/10, p. 30:4-5. R.D. stated that he "was looking more at the money [in the cash register] than [he] was the gunman." Id. at p. 56:21 – p. 57:9. After T.M. turned from the window to walk away, R.D. testified that his attention was focused only on getting the license plate number of the vehicle and using the telephone to call the police. Id. at p. 36:6-9. Therefore, R.D.'s degree of attention on the driver of the vehicle was minimal, at best.

c.   *R.D.'s accuracy of prior description of Petitioner.*

In this case, R.D.'s description of the driver was extremely generic. R.D. stated that the driver was thin, black female and had a ponytail. R.T., 10/19/10, p. 35:16-17; Id. at p. 78:17-18. R.D.'s accuracy is irrelevant because of the vast number of individual who meet that description.

Even upon the police showing R.D. a photograph line-up with Petitioner's picture, the police told R.D. to pick a person who "could have been" involved in the robbery. R.T., 10/19/10, p. 42:9-13. After receiving that improper instruction, R.D. testified that he picked someone he "thought --- it could look more **like the person** that was driving." Id. at p. 44:2-5. R.D. did not state it *was* the person driving the vehicle. In fact, a couple of questions after this, R.D. informed the jury that he did not recognize "anybody in [the] courtroom who [he could] say for sure was involved in this armed robbery." Id. at p. 44:12-15. Nor did he see anyone in the courtroom that "match[ed] the description of somebody who was involved in this armed robbery." Id. at p. 44:16-19.

d.   *R.D.'s level of certainty at the confrontation.*

The following exchange between defense counsel and R.D. shows that R.D.'s level of certainty was nil:

DEFENSE COUNSEL: Now, isn't it also fair to say that when you first talked to the police, you said you were unsure if you'd be able to identify?

R.D.: Yes.

DEFENSE COUNSEL: Okay. Because you didn't get a long look, correct?

R.D.: Yes." R.T., 10/19/10, p. 60:3-9.

R.D. also stated that when he was shown the line-up photographs he was not "sure if this was the person driving that car at all." Id. at p. 60: 14-19. If fact, during trial, R.D. admitted that he did not know if Petitioner was the person who was involved in the robbery. Id. at p. 60:23 – p. 61:3. Thus, R.D.'s level of certainty was non-existent; R.D. was not certain of who the driver of the vehicle was.

e.   *Amount of time between crime and the confrontation.*

The offense in this case took place on March 14, 2008. ROA 1. The photograph line-up took place on March 15, 2008. R.T., 10/19/10, p. 41:19-25. R.D.'s in-court identification took place over two years later in October, 2010.

In examining the above factors, R.D.'s identification was unreliable. As such, defense counsel should have challenged the identification. His failure to do so amounted to deficient performance as contemplated by *Strickland*.

Prejudice to Petitioner

Had defense counsel challenged R.D.'s identification of Petitioner, the above analysis shows that he would have prevailed on that motion. Had he done so, then R.D. would not have been permitted to identify Petitioner in court. Because this case hinges solely upon R.D.'s identification of Petitioner, without that identification, the jury would have acquitted Petitioner. Therefore, Petitioner suffered prejudice by defense counsel failing to file the motion to challenge the identification in this matter.

C.   Petitioner is entitled to an evidentiary hearing.

Petitioner has the burden of proving the allegations in this petition by a preponderance of the evidence. Rule 32.8(c); *State v. Verdugo*, 183 Ariz. 135, 901 P.2d 1165 (1995). Petitioner has met that burden. In the alternative, Petitioner should be granted a hearing on the claims presented herein. To deprive Petitioner of a hearing under these unique and compelling circumstances would deny Petitioner due process of law under the United States and Arizona Constitutions. *United States v. Schaflander*, 743 F.2d 714 (9th Cir. 1984). Factual and legal issues must be resolved by the Court at a plenary hearing, and it may summarily deny a Petition only when it conclusively determines there are absolutely no materials issues of fact or law in dispute. Rule 32.6(c), Arizona Rules of Criminal Procedure.

The proper inquiry in this regard concerns whether, "if appellant's contentions are taken as true, do they successfully show ineffective assistance of counsel?" *State v. Suarez*, 23 Ariz.App. 45, 530 P.2d 402 (1975). The Arizona Supreme Court has held that a petitioner is invariably entitled to an evidentiary hearing where a colorable claim – one that, "if the defendant's allegations are true, might have changed the outcome" – is presented. *State v. Spreitz*, 202 Ariz. 1, 39 P.3d 525 (2002)(en banc), citing *State v. Watton*, 164 Ariz. at 328, 793 P.2d at 85, citing *State v. Schrock*, 149 Ariz. 433, 441, 719 P.2d 1049, 1057 (1986). "A petitioner need not provide detailed evidence, but must provide specific factual allegations that, if true, would entitle him to relief." *United States v. Hearst*, 638 F.2d 1190, 1194 (9th Cir. 1980).

The Court at this stage must assume all of Petitioner's claims to be true, and make its determination as to whether a hearing is warranted based strictly upon that assumption. *State v. Fillmore*, 187 Ariz. 174, 927 P.2d 1303 (1996). Assuming the facts stated herein to be true, Petitioner has provided colorable claims of ineffective assistance of counsel and violations of her due process rights.

IV.

CONCLUSION

Petitioner respectfully requests that this Court find that trial counsel provided ineffective assistance of counsel and vacate her conviction and sentence.

RESPECTFULLY SUBMITTED this   day of   ,   .

THE HOPKINS LAW OFFICE, P.C.

/s/_____

Cedric Martin Hopkins, Esq.
Attorney for Petitioner

FORM #6

NAME: _____
ADDRESS:_____
_____
_____
(ACTING PRO PER)

IN THE SUPERIOR COURT OF ARIZONA
IN AND FOR THE COUNTY OF _____

STATE OF ARIZONA,	Case No.: _____
Plaintiff,	
v.	**DECLARATION OF DEFENDANT:**
_____,	_____
Defendant.	Hon. _____

Pursuant to Rule 32.5 of the Arizona Rules of Criminal Procedure, Defendant

_____ hereby declares, under penalty of perjury that the information

contained in the Pro Per Petition for Post-Conviction Relief mailed on the ____ day of

_____, 20____, is true to the best of his knowledge and belief and contains all

grounds for relief under Rule 32.1.

      RESPECTFULLY SUBMITTED this ____ day of _____, 20___.

_____
Defendant, Acting Pro Per

FORM #7

NAME: _____

ADDRESS:_____

_____

_____

(ACTING PRO PER)

IN THE SUPERIOR COURT OF ARIZONA
IN AND FOR THE COUNTY OF _____

STATE OF ARIZONA,	Case No.: _____
Plaintiff,	
v.	**MOTION TO EXTEND TIME TO FILE PRO PER PETITION FOR POST-CONVICTION RELIEF**
_____,	
Defendant.	Hon. _____

COMES NOW, the Defendant, _____, acting pro per, and

respectfully requests that this Court extend the time to file the pro per petition for

post-conviction relief. This basis for this motion is as follows:

_____

_____

_____

_____

_____

_____

_____

RESPECTFULLY SUBMITTED this ____ day of _____, 20__.

_____

Name:

Defendant, Acting Pro Per

FORM #8a

THE HOPKINS LAW OFFICE, P.C.
10645 N. Oracle Rd., #121-326
Tucson, Arizona 85737
Telephone: 520.465.2658
Facsimile: 520.867.6509
objectionyourhonor@hotmail.com

Cedric Martin Hopkins, Esq.
California State Bar No. 226313
Arizona State Bar No. 22790
Pima Co. Bar No. 65828

IN THE SUPERIOR COURT OF THE STATE OF ARIZONA

IN AND FOR THE COUNTY OF MARICOPA

STATE OF ARIZONA,
 	
         Plaintiff,
v.
 	
DBR (001),
 	
         Defendant.
	Case Number: CRXXXX-XXXXXX-XXX DT
	
	MOTION TO STAY RULE 32 PROCEEDINGS
	
	Hon. XXXX XXXXX

Counsel for Petitioner, DBR, moves this Court for an order staying the current

Rule 32 proceedings. The basis for this request is as follows:

The Court of Appeals' Memorandum Decision (filed 7/18/2013) in Defendant's

case vacated this Court's February 12, 2010 order and reinstated this Court's July 17,

2009 order. After his petition for review to the Arizona Supreme Court was

unsuccessful, Defendant filed a "Motion for Court Orders Pursuant to Court of Appeals

Mandate" on June 19, 2014 (dated June 9, 2014). The defendant also requested to

reinstate his Rule 32 proceedings. The defendant's motion was filed prior to this Court

reinstating his Rule 32 proceedings and appointing him counsel.

Undersigned counsel is requesting that the Rule 32 proceedings be stayed so that

this Court can issue an order reinstating this Court's July 17, 2009 order and, more

importantly, rule on the defendant's June 19, 2014 motion, which again, was filed prior to the reinstatement of these Rule 32 proceedings. As it is, the Arizona Department of Corrections has not complied with the Court of Appeals' Memorandum Decision for the stated reason that the Department needs an order from the Maricopa County Superior Court that the July 17, 2009 order is controlling. Without that order, the Court of Appeals' instructions regarding the defendant's sentence are going disregarded.

Based on the foregoing, undersigned counsel respectfully requests that this Court stay the Rule 32 proceedings so that the defendant's June 19, 2014 motion can be ruled upon. Following this Court ruling upon the defendant's June 19, 2014 motion, undersigned counsel respectfully requests that this Court reinstate the Rule 32 proceedings.

RESPECTFULLY SUBMITTED this XX day of XXXXXXX, XXXX.

THE HOPKINS LAW OFFICE, P.C.
/s/_____/
Cedric Martin Hopkins, Esq.
Attorney for Petitioner

FORM #8b

NAME: _____

ADDRESS:_____

_____

_____

(ACTING PRO PER)

IN THE SUPERIOR COURT OF ARIZONA
IN AND FOR THE COUNTY OF _____

STATE OF ARIZONA,

     Plaintiff,

v.

_____,

     Defendant.

Case No.: _____

MOTION TO STAY RULE 32 PROCEEDINGS

Hon. _____

COMES NOW, the Defendant, _____, acting pro per, and respectfully requests that this Court stay the current Rule 32 proceedings pending in the above-captioned case. This basis for this motion is as follows:

_____

_____

_____

_____

_____

_____

_____

RESPECTFULLY SUBMITTED this ____ day of _____, 20__.

_____

Name:

Defendant, Acting Pro Per

FORM #9a

THE HOPKINS LAW OFFICE, P.C.
10645 N. Oracle Rd., #121-326
Tucson, Arizona 85737
Telephone: 520.465.2658
Facsimile: 520.867.6509
objectionyourhonor@hotmail.com

Cedric Martin Hopkins, Esq.
California State Bar No. 226313
Arizona State Bar No. 22790
Pima Co. Bar No. 65828

IN THE SUPERIOR COURT OF THE STATE OF ARIZONA

IN AND FOR THE COUNTY OF MARICOPA

STATE OF ARIZONA,
 	
     Plaintiff,
 	
v.
 	
SDR (001),
 	
     Defendant.
	Case Number: CRXXXX-XXXXXX-XXX DT
	
	MOTION TO DISMISS RULE 32 PROCEEDINGS WITHOUT PREJUDICE
	
	Hon. XXXX XXXXX

Undersigned counsel moves this Court for an order dismissing the Rule 32 proceedings without prejudice. Defendant's appellate case (1 CA-CR XX-XXXX) is currently pending before the Court of Appeals. All briefs have been filed and the Court of Appeals took the matter under advisement on XX-XX-XXXX.

As such, Defendant respectfully requests that this Court dismiss Defendant's Rule 32 proceedings until her appellate proceedings are completed and the Court of Appeals has issued its mandate.

    RESPECTFULLY SUBMITTED this XX day of XXXXXX, XXXX.
        THE HOPKINS LAW OFFICE, P.C.

        /s/ Cedric Hopkins
        Cedric Martin Hopkins, Esq.
        Attorney for Defendant

FORM #10

Fax to: 602/506-3609

This form must be used to request expert witness fees, tape transcription fees, travel expenses for investigators, mitigation specialists and witnesses, and any other expenses paid by the Maricopa County Office of Contract Counsel.

PRO PER CASE?

☐ YES   ☐ NO

Attorney Name:	Date Requested:
Attorney Phone:	Attorney Fax No:
Name of Client:	Case No.:
Charges:	

TYPE OF REQUEST

☐ Investigator
(Appt'd on Rotation Basis)

☐ Mitigation Specialist

☐ Expert Witness

☐ Tape Transcripts

☐ Investigation travel
(Attach Travel info. Form)

☐ Mitigation travel
(Attach Travel info. Form)

☐ Witness Travel
(Attach Travel info. Form)

☐ Process Service
(See instructions at bottom of ROF)

☐ Other

Requested Vendor:_____
(MANDATORY)
Estimate dollar amount or number of hours requested:_____
(MANDATORY)
Rationale for Request:_____
(MANDATORY)
_____
_____
_____

****

AUTHORIZATION

Approval is only good for six months from the date of approval. If the expenditure expires, funding must be requested again. If any expenditure is incurred after an approved funding request has expired, Maricopa County will not honor or ratify any billing for the service rendered.

Approved _____   Denied _____

_____
OCC Authorized Signature   Date

Investigator/Mitigation Specialist Assigned:_____

Special Conditions.: _____
_____

A COPY OF THIS FORM MUST ACCOMPANY ANY BILLING PURSUANT TO THIS MATTER.

Process Service: Forward all subpoenas requiring service along with an approved ROF via e-mail attachment to subpoenas@mail.maricopa.gov. Subpoenas should NOT be delivered to OPDS.

Maricopa County Office of Contract Counsel

FORM #11

SPECIFICATION FOR REQUESTED **ANCILLARY** FEES

Office of Court Appointed Counsel 33 N. Stone Ave. 19th Floor, Suite 1905   Tucson, AZ. 85701

Fax: 520-724-4466

(*This document is confidential and will be used for the sole purpose of determining the **NEED AND REASONABLENESS** of fees & assessments)

Name of Attorney: _____   Request Date: _____

Attorney Phone: _____   Return Fax No.: _____

Email: _____   Appointment Date: _____

Defendant: _____   Case Number: _____

Custody Status: _____   Is Defendant a Spanish speaker: _____

Class & Charge Description: _____   Judge/Div: _____

Class & Charge Description: _____

☐ Felony ☐ FD Murder ☐ Death Penalty ☐ Juvenile ☐ Misdemeanor ☐ Appeal ☐ Rule 32

If Rule 32: From COP _____   Trial (# of days) _____

Have you requested a Settlement Conference? _____

Present Case Status _____

Are there co-defendants? If so, how many? _____

Type of Expense (investigator, paralegal, expert/type, transcriber): _____

Vendor Name: _____   Vendor Rate: _____

No. of Hours Requested _____   Request No. _____

Please provide brief factual synopsis of your case to allow us to evaluate your need.

_____

_____

_____

Describe the work that **needs to be performed** and the **reason** the performance of this work will help in the defense of your case.

_____

_____

_____

_____

_____

_____   _____
Attorney Signature   Date

☐ Approved   ☐ Denied

_____
Office of Court-Appointed Counsel

Special Conditions: _____

A copy of this form **must** accompany any billing pursuant to this matter. All **new** vendors must register with Pima County at https://vendor.pima.gov/webapp/VSSPROD1/Advantage. Call (520) 724-3021 or (520) 724-8465 for assistance with registration.

FORM #12

IN THE COURT OF APPEALS

STATE OF ARIZONA

DIVISION ONE

STATE OF ARIZONA,	)	Court of Appeals Case No.:
	)	XXXX-XXXX
Respondent,	)	
	)	
vs.	)	Maricopa County Superior
	)	Court Case No.:
R.H.,	)	CRXXXX-XXXXXX
	)	
Petitioner.	)	
_____	)	

PETITION FOR REVIEW
(DENIAL OF PETITION FOR POST-CONVICTION RELIEF)

THE HOPKINS LAW OFFICE, P.C.

Cedric Martin Hopkins
10645 N. Oracle Rd., #121-326
Tucson, Arizona 85737
Phone: 520.465.2658
objectionyourhonor@hotmail.com
AZ Bar No. 22790
Attorney for R.H.

TABLE OF CONTENTS

TABLE OF CITATIONS

CASES

CONSTITUTIONS

ARIZONA RULES OF CRIMINAL PROCEDURE

RULES OF PROFESSIONAL RESPONSIBILITY

STATEMENT OF THE MATERIAL FACTS

¶1   The State of Arizona charged Petitioner with three counts of Aggravated Assault, class three felonies, and five counts of Kidnapping, class two felonies. (Indictment, 05/06/93). Prior to proceeding to trial, Petitioner was offered a plea agreement by the State. Exhibit A, Plea Agreement, undated.[3] After a brief meeting with his attorney, he chose to reject the plea agreement.

¶2   G.G. (trial counsel) represented Petitioner with respect to the trial and sentencing. Exhibit B, Affidavit of R.H. The State offered Petitioner a plea agreement. Id. Trial counsel delivered the plea agreement to Petitioner but did not explain the terms of the plea agreement. Id. The meeting between Petitioner and trial counsel lasted less than two minutes. Id. During that meeting, trial counsel explained that he did not have much time to meet with Petitioner because trial counsel had over 100 cases he was handling at that time and needed to meet with other inmates at the jail. Id.

¶3   During the fleeting meeting, trial counsel did not explain the difference between pleading guilty versus pleading "no contest," or why "no contest" was marked out on his plea agreement. Id. Trial counsel did not

---

[3] All exhibit references are to those exhibits filed with the petition for post-conviction relief.

explain to Petitioner the prison term he faced under the plea agreement as compared to the prison terms he faced if found guilty at trial. Id. At no point did trial counsel articulate the total number of years Petitioner was facing if he went to trial and was found guilty. Id. Trial counsel did not explain to Petitioner that the sentencing judge would be forced to sentence Petitioner to consecutive terms of prison for his charges under the indictment if the jury found him guilty. Id. Petitioner understood the plea to have a maximum prison term of 21 years and his prison exposure if he was found guilt at trial to be the same. Id.

¶4 Had the plea agreement been explained properly—including Petitioner only being exposed to a total of 21 years in prison under the plea agreement—Petitioner would have accepted the agreement and not elected to have a jury trial. Id. The reason Petitioner did not accept the plea agreement is because he felt that he could be sentenced to the same prison sentence under the plea agreement as he would if he was found guilty at trial. Id. Trial counsel did not instruct Petitioner that he actually faced significantly more prison time if Petitioner did not accept the plea agreement and was found guilty at trial. Id.

¶5 After being found guilty at trial, Petitioner exhausted his remedies under Rule 31 with his direct appeal. Id. Thereafter, the Court first appointed N.B. to represent Petitioner for his post-conviction relief proceedings. Id. N.B. represented Petitioner's co-defendant, however, and moved to withdraw. Id. The Court then appointed attorney R.D. to represent Petitioner for his post-conviction relief proceedings under Rule 32. Id. At that time, R.D. worked for the Maricopa County Public Defender's Office. Id. R.D. filed a pleading with the Court indicating that he did not find any viable issues under Rule 32. Id.

¶6   After exercising his right to a jury trial on the charges, Petitioner was found guilty of three counts of Aggravated Assault, all class three dangerous felonies, and four counts of Kidnapping, all class two dangerous felonies. The Court then sentenced Petitioner to a total of 80.5 years in prison by running the terms of imprisonment consecutive to one another.

¶7   Petitioner filed a petition for post-conviction, which the trial court dismissed without providing any analysis or holding an evidentiary hearing. (Attachment A, Lower Court Ruling, dated 12/28/12, filed 01/02/13). Petitioner then filed a Motion for Rehearing requesting that the trial court provide its reasoning for dismissing the petition, which the trial court also denied. (Attachment B, Lower Court Ruling, dated 01/17/13, filed 01/24/13).

ISSUES PRESENTED FOR REVIEW

A.   Whether a conflict of interest existed between trial counsel and first post-conviction relief counsel that entitles Petitioner to file a petition for post-conviction relief as though it is his initial post-conviction proceeding.

B.   Whether defense counsel provided ineffective assistance of counsel in failing to properly inform Petitioner regarding the plea agreement that was offered by the State.

C.   Whether the *Frye* and *Lafler* cases constitute a significant change in the law.

D.   Whether Petitioner is entitled to an evidentiary hearing on the claims that he presented to the trial court.

ARGUMENT

¶8   At the outset it should be noted that the trial court failed to provide any reasoning for its denial of the petition for post-conviction relief. The trial court simply issued a one-sentence order summarily dismissing the petition. Petitioner filed a motion for rehearing specifically requesting that the trial court provide analysis and/or reasoning for denying Petitioner's claims. Because the trial court failed to provide such reasoning, Petitioner's claims are largely identical to the claims he presented in the original petition for post-conviction relief. While Petitioner understands that this Court frowns upon such "cut-and-paste" briefs, Petitioner was not given any analysis for the denial of his original claims. Petitioner respectfully requests that this Court not issue a summary order.

¶9   Summary orders are appropriate, "where the trial court clearly and correctly articulate[d] its ruling..." *State v. Whipple*, 177 Ariz. 272, 273, 866 P.2d 1358,1359 (1993). The Court of Appeals' summary orders are proper in those circumstances because of the "look through" rule that the United States Supreme Court has implemented. The "look through" rule allows courts to look "to the last *explained* decision to determine whether a habeas corpus petitioner has litigated his claim on the merits in state court." Id. at 273-74, 866 P.2d at 1359-60, citing *Ylst v. Nunnemaker*, 501 U.S. 797, 111 S.Ct. 2590, 2594-95, 115 L.Ed.2d 706 (1991) and *Coleman v. Thompson*, 501 U.S. 722, 111 S.Ct. 2546, 2559, 115 L.Ed.2d 640 (1991) (emphasis in original).

¶10   The trial court's unexplained ruling denying Petitioner's petition for post-conviction relief does not permit this Court, or any other court—State or Federal—to "look through" to make determinations regarding Petitioner's claims. Such an unexplained ruling will make unclear whether or not Petitioner's claims are subject to a state procedural default, either expressed or implied. *Robinson v. Schriro*, 595 F.3d 1086, 1100 (9th Cir. 2010), *citing Boyd v. Thompson*, 147 F.3d 1124, 1126 (9th Circ. 1998). Such ambiguity may cause his federal claims under 28 U.S.C. § 2254 to be precluded.

Wainwright v. Sykes, 433 U.S. 72, 80-88, 97 S.Ct. 2497, 2503-2507, 53

L.Ed.2d 594 (1977).

     A.   **A conflict of interest existed between trial counsel and first post-conviction relief counsel that entitles Petitioner to file a petition for post-conviction relief as though it is his initial post-conviction proceeding.**

¶11   For trial, the Court appointed the Maricopa County Public Defender's Office to represent Petitioner. G.G. (now deceased) was the attorney from the Public Defender's Office who represented Petitioner at trial. The Court then appointed another attorney—R.D.—to represent Petitioner for his first post-conviction proceedings under Rule 32, Ariz.R.Crim.Proc. Both, attorney G.G. and attorney R.D., worked for the Maricopa County Public Defender's Office. G.G. worked for the Public Defender's Office while he represented Petitioner and R.D. had previously worked for the Public Defender's Office at the time he represented Petitioner.

¶12   Because G.G. and R.D. worked for the same office, and R.D. reviewed G.G.'s work, it was incumbent upon G.G. to receive an executed consent from Petitioner, after informing Petitioner of the conflict of interest. Absent from the court record or trial file is such consent from Petitioner permitting the unequivocal conflict of interest that existed between R.D. and G.G..

¶13   Arizona courts, as well as the State Bar of Arizona, have long decided that the type of conflict between R.D. and G.G. is not permitted without the client's permission. In *State v. Marrow*, the Arizona Supreme Court explained it this way: the "standard for determining whether counsel was reasonably effective is 'an objective' standard which we feel can best be developed by someone other than the person responsible for the conduct." *Marlow*, 163 Ariz. 65, 68, 786 P.2d 395, 398 (1989) (quoting *Strickland v. Washington*, 466 U.S. 668, 688, 104 S.Ct. 2052, 80 L.Ed.2d 674 (1984)).

¶14   The State Bar of Arizona agrees with the *Marlow* court and explains their Rule further:

> "While lawyers are associated in a firm, none of them shall knowingly represent a client when any one of them practicing alone would be prohibited from doing so by ERs 1.7 or 1.9, unless the prohibition is based on a personal interest of the prohibited lawyer and does not present a significant risk of materially limiting the representation of the client by the remaining lawyers in the firm." Arizona Rules of Professional Conduct, E.R. 1.10(a): Imputation of Conflicts of Interest.

As the *Marlow* court points out, having two attorneys from the same office would limit the representation explained in E.R. 1.10(a). Such limitation of representation is the State Bar of Arizona's underpinning to prohibiting this type of conflict.

¶15 The Rules of Professional Conduct for Arizona lawyers makes it clear that "a lawyer shall not represent a client if the representation involves a concurrent conflict of interest." E.R. 1.7. In the comment to E.R. 1.7, the State Bar of Arizona gives its rationale for the rule. "Loyalty and independent judgment are essential elements in the lawyer's relationship to a client." E.R. 1.7, Comment [1].

¶16 In the instant case, R.D. reviewed Petitioner's file and determined that no credible issue existed to raise on Petitioner's behalf. Petitioner, acting *pro per*, filed a petition for post-conviction relief with the court that outlined issues the court deemed not only credible, but warranted an evidentiary hearing. This fact suggests that the safeguards outlined in *Marlow* and E.R. 1.7 and 1.10(a), were not adhered to in Petitioner's case. R.D.'s "loyalty" highlighted by Comment [1] to E.R. 1.7 is called into question as he failed to find any fault—whatsoever—with his previous employer, yet Petitioner did so to a point that the Court recognized that his *pro per* claims against R.D.'s former employer were credible.

¶17 Also explained in E.R. 1.7, is the fact that in order for R.D. to have represented Petitioner in a case against his former employee, he would have to get Petitioner's informed consent. No such consent was given in this case. Petitioner should be able to file a conflict-free initial petition.

B. **Defense counsel provided ineffective assistance of counsel in failing to properly inform Petitioner regarding the plea agreement that was offered by the State.**

¶18   Prior to commencing his trial, Petitioner was offered a plea agreement by the State. Trial counsel (G.G.) brought the plea agreement to the jail where Petitioner was being housed. G.G. met with Petitioner for less than two minutes; just enough time to give him the plea agreement and ask Petitioner if he wanted to sign it. See, Exhibit B. At no time during that meeting did G.G. explain the terms of the plea agreement to Petitioner. Id. G.G. simply asked Petitioner if he wanted to sign the plea agreement. Id. Petitioner, seeing what he believed was the same prison term exposure in the plea agreement as what he would receive if he lost at trial (21 years), informed G.G. that he did not want to accept the plea agreement. Id. No further discussion was had on the plea agreement. Id. G.G. informed Petitioner that he had over 100 cases and that he needed to meet with other inmates at the jail—that was the extent of G.G.'s communication of the plea agreement terms to Petitioner. Id.

¶19   To prove ineffective assistance of counsel, a petitioner must show that counsel's representation fell below the standard of care in the profession and that the petitioner was prejudiced. *Strickland v. Washington*, 466 U.S. 668 (1984)(both prongs of test must be satisfied); *State v. Walton*, 159 Ariz. 571,

769 P.2d 1017 (1989); U.S. Const. Amends. 5, 6 & 14; Ariz. Const., Art. 2 §§ 4 &24.

¶20   Defendants have a Sixth Amendment right to counsel, a right that, according to the United States Supreme Court, extends to the plea-bargaining process. *Missouri v. Frye*, — U.S. —, 132 S.Ct. 1399 (2012) citing, *Padilla v . Kentucky*, 559 U.S. ——, ——, 130 S.Ct. 1473, 1486, 176 L.Ed.2d 284 (2010) and *Hill v. Lockhart*, 474 U.S. 52, 57, 106 S.Ct. 366, 370, 88 L.Ed.2d 203 (1985). The Supreme Court has now decided that defendants are "entitled to the effective assistance of competent counsel" during the plea negotiations phase of their cases. *Frye, supra,* and *Lafler v. Cooper*, — U.S. —, 132 S.Ct. 1376 (2012). In *Frye* and *Lafler*, the Court held that the test for ineffective assistance of counsel under *Strickland v. Washington* now applies to challenges to guilty pleas.

Deficient Performance

¶21   In *Frye*, the issue before the Court with respect to the deficient performance arm of the two-part *Strickland* test was "whether defense counsel has the duty to communicate the terms of a formal offer to accept a plea on terms and conditions that may result in a lesser sentence, a conviction on lesser charges, or both." *Frye* at 1408. The Court answered that inquiry in the affirmative. Id.

¶22 As shown above, G.G. failed to communicate the terms of the plea agreement to Petitioner. Most importantly, G.G. did not communicate to Petitioner his exposure of consecutive prison sentences if he lost at trial. That lack of communication proved to be fatal. As Petitioner sat in the jail and reviewed the plea agreement during that 120-second meeting, he was deciding between life and death, nothing less. Under the terms of the plea agreement, Petitioner would have had to serve two-thirds of a 21-year prison term—or 14 years—at the most. At the other end of the spectrum, Petitioner's exposure at trial was potentially over 100 years, to which he was actually sentenced to serve 80.5 years in prison.

Importance of the Record

¶23 The *Frye* Court examined the court record with respect to the deficient performance prong of the *Strickland* test. The *Frye* Court found it instructive that the "record is void of any evidence of any effort by trial counsel to communicate the [formal] Offer to Frye during the Offer window, let alone any evidence that Frye's conduct interfered with trial counsel's ability to do so." *Frye*, 132 S.Ct. at 1410.

¶24 In Petitioner's case, nothing in the court record or trial file shows that G.G. properly communicated the terms of the plea agreement. The opposite is true. G.G.'s performance with respect to communicating the terms of the plea agreement amounted to a less than two-minute meeting with Petitioner and a total failure to explain essential aspects of the plea agreement; aspects that would have had Petitioner leaving the prison years ago versus being 110 years old upon his release.

¶25   What intensifies G.G.'s deficient performance even more is the fact that Petitioner repeatedly attempted to reach G.G. to discuss his case, to no avail. Petitioner kept detailed notes of the telephone calls he made to G.G.'s office. Exhibit C, Petitioner's Hand-Written Notes Re: Attempted Telephone Calls. Each of those telephone calls were unreturned by G.G..

¶26   Just as in *Frye*, the record in Petitioner's case lacks any evidence that G.G. properly communicated the terms of the plea agreement to Petitioner. Therefore, just as in *Frye*, nothing in the record suggests that the terms of the plea agreement were communicated to Petitioner.

¶27   Equally important as to what was in the plea agreement that was not explained to Petitioner is what is not contained in the plea agreement that was not explained to Petitioner. The plea agreement ensures that Petitioner would receive concurrent terms of prison for all counts that he would plead guilty to. What Petitioner did not know, and what G.G. did not communicate, is that if Petitioner was found guilty, then the sentencing judge would have no choice but to sentence him to consecutive prison terms for the counts that he would be found guilty of. G.G. breached his duty to communicate the terms of the plea agreement, which, as the *Frye* Court instructs, qualifies as deficient performance.

Prejudice Prong of Strickland

¶28   In *Frye*, the United States Supreme Court articulated a three-part test to determine if a defendant has been prejudiced by trial counsel's deficient performance during plea negotiations. First, in order for a defendant "[t]o show prejudice from ineffective assistance of counsel where a plea offer has lapsed or been rejected because of counsel's deficient performance, defendants must demonstrate a reasonable probability they would have accepted the earlier plea offer had they been afforded effective assistance of counsel." *Frye*, 132 S.Ct. at 1409.

¶29   Unequivocally, Petitioner would have chosen to serve 14 years in prison as compared to serving 80.5 years in prison. Even more convincing, Petitioner would not have risked a possible prison sentence totaling over 100 years verses accepting a plea agreement that maxed out his prison term to 14 years. There is no question that Petitioner would have accepted the plea agreement offered by the State in this case. Indeed, that principle is the benchmark of these entire current proceedings before this Court. Had G.G. communicated the terms of the plea agreement to Petitioner, he would have accepted the plea agreement—and it's significant and life-changing benefits—and not proceeded to trial with an exposure of over 100 years in prison. *See*, Exhibit B.

¶30   Secondly, in order for defendant to show prejudice, they "must also demonstrate a reasonable probability the plea would have been entered without the prosecution canceling it or the trial court refusing to accept it, if they had the authority to exercise that discretion under state law." *Frye*, 132 S.Ct. at 1409. And under Arizona law, contract law governs plea agreements. *Coy v. Fields*, 200 Ariz. 442, 445, ¶9, 27 P.3d 799, 802 (App.2001). Therefore, once the State extends an offer to resolve the case by a plea agreement, and the defendant accepts that agreement, the State cannot withdraw from the agreement absent a showing of fraud, mistake or any other issue authorized by contract law. *See, Malcoff v. Coyier*, 14 Ariz.App. 524, 526, 484 P.2d 1053, 1055 (1971)

¶31   In Petitioner's case, the State would not have had the power to cancel or withdraw the plea agreement after Petitioner accepted it. And there is no indication that any fraud, mistake or duress would have existed in Petitioner's case.

¶32   Moreover, the fact that Petitioner's co-defendant received a more favorable plea agreement than Petitioner, and the Court accepted that agreement, it follows that Petitioner's plea agreement would have been accepted by the Court, as well.

¶33   And most importantly, the prosecutor in Petitioner's case signed the plea agreement, indicating the plea was appropriate.[4] See, Exhibit A.

¶34   Finally, "it is necessary to show a reasonable probability that the end result of the criminal process would have been more favorable by reason of a plea to a lesser charge or a sentence of less prison time." *Frye*, 132 S.Ct. at 1409, *citing, Glover v. United States*, 531 U.S. 198, 203, 121 S.Ct. 696, 148 L.Ed.2d 604 (2001) ("[A]ny amount of [additional] jail time has Sixth Amendment significance"). As stated in *Lafler*, a defendant must show that the terms of the plea agreement "would have been less severe than under the judgment and sentence that in fact were imposed." *Lafler*, 132 S.Ct. at 1385.

¶35   In *Lafler*, just as in Petitioner's case, the defendant elected to reject the plea agreement and proceed to trial. The defendant in *Lafler* received a more severe sentence that was "3 1/2 times more severe than he likely would have received by pleading guilty." Id.

---

[4] The language above the prosecutor's signature states, "I have reviewed this matter and concur that the plea and disposition set forth herein are appropriate and are in the interests of justice." Exhibit A.

¶36   After being found guilty at trial, Petitioner was sentenced to 80.5 years in prison. The trial judge sentenced Petitioner to consecutive terms of prison, which included dangerous nature allegations to those charges.

¶37   The plea agreement extended to Petitioner, on the other hand, required him to serve two-thirds of a 21 year prison term, or 14 years, at the most. That plea agreement also removed the dangerous nature of the charges, along with removing the dangerous crimes against children allegation. The plea agreement also stipulates that all of the prison terms would be served concurrent to one another.

¶38   As compared to the defendant's sentence in *Lafler* being 3 ½ times more severe by proceeding to trial instead of accepting the plea agreement, **Petitioner's current prison sentence is 5 ¾ times as severe** as the amount of prison time he would have received under the plea agreement. According to the *Lafler* Court, Petitioner has shown prejudice in this regard.

¶39   As shown above, G.G.'s performance during plea negotiations was deficient in that he did not communicate the terms of the plea agreement. Petitioner was prejudiced by G.G.'s deficient performance in that he rejected the unexplained plea agreement and elected to go to trial and received a substantially more severe prison sentence than he would have under the plea agreement.

Remedy

¶40   The *Lafler* Court stated that the "Sixth Amendment remedies should be 'tailored to the injury suffered from the constitutional violation and should not unnecessarily infringe on competing interests.'" *Lafler*, 132 S.Ct. at 1388-89, *citing United States v. Morrison*, 449 U.S. 361, 364, 101 S.Ct. 665, 66 L.Ed.2d 564 (1981). "Thus, a remedy must 'neutralize the taint' of a constitutional violation, while at the same time not grant a windfall to the defendant or needlessly squander the considerable resources the State properly invested in the criminal prosecution." Id. *citing Morrison*, 449 U.S. at 365, 101 S.Ct. 665

¶41   The *Lafler* Court went on to explain that two possible remedies are available to this Court in Petitioner's situation. First, the Court stated that a resentencing might suffice to remedy the violation if there is no difference in the charges the defendant was convicted of at trial as compared to the charges in the plea agreement. Id. The resentencing option is proper when the prison sentence is at issue.

¶42   On the other hand, the *Lafler* Court explained that a second option is available when the plea agreement extended by the State "was for a guilty plea to a count or counts less serious than the ones for which a defendant was convicted after trial, or if a mandatory sentence confines a judge's sentencing discretion after trial." *Lafler*, 132 S.Ct. at 1389. In that instance, "a resentencing based on the conviction at trial may not suffice." Id. The *Lafler* Court instructed that in these situations, "the proper exercise of discretion to remedy the constitutional injury may be to require the prosecution to reoffer the plea proposal." Id.

¶43   Because the State extended to Petitioner a plea agreement that was for less serious counts and a mandatory sentence that restricted the sentencing judge's discretion, the option most appropriate to cure the constitutional violation is to order the reoffering of the plea agreement to Petitioner. In the alternative, if this Court does not feel that the reoffering of the plea agreement is appropriate, then Petitioner respectfully requests that this Court resentence him under the terms of the plea agreement.

C.   **The *Frye* and *Lafler* cases constitute a significant change in the law.**

¶44   Petitioner brings this action under Rule 32.1(g), alleging a significant change in the law. Specifically, Petitioner asserts that the United States Supreme Court cases in *Frye* and *Lafler*, *supra*, constitute a significant change in the law and that those cases apply to his case. The language used by the Supreme Court in *Frye* supports Petitioner's contention:

> "This Court **now holds** that, as a general rule, defense counsel has the duty to communicate formal offers from the prosecution to accept a plea on terms and conditions that may be favorable

to the accused. When defense counsel allowed the offer to expire without advising the defendant or allowing him to consider it, defense counsel did not render the effective assistance the Constitution requires." *Frye*, 132 S.Ct. at 1408.

¶45 Arizona permits post-conviction relief if "[t]here has been a significant change in the law that if determined to apply to defendant's case would probably overturn the defendant's conviction or sentence." Rule 32.1(g), Ariz.R.Crim.Proc. In Petitioner's case, as shown above, G.G. rendered ineffective assistance of counsel by failing to communicate the terms of the plea agreement. Both *Frye* and *Lafler*, if applied to Petitioner's case, instruct that Petitioner now has a remedy available to him of reinstating the original plea agreement offer. Therefore, there has been a significant change in the law that, if applied to Petitioner's case, would overturn his conviction and sentence, as explained above.

¶46 And in what appears to be somewhat of a preemptive strike, the *Lafler* Court explained that applying the principles outlined in Petitioner's petition for post-conviction relief would not "open the floodgates to litigation by defendants seeking to unsettle their convictions." *Lafler*, 132 S.Ct. at 1389. As such, the recent United States Supreme Court decisions in *Frye* and *Lafler* constitute a significant change in the law and, as explained in *Lafler*, apply to Petitioner's circumstances.

D. Petitioner was entitled to an evidentiary hearing on the claims submitted in his petition for post-conviction relief.

¶47 The Arizona Supreme Court has held that a petitioner is invariably entitled to an evidentiary hearing where a colorable claim – one that, "if the defendant's allegations are true, might have changed the outcome" – is presented. *State v. Spreitz*, 202 Ariz. 1, 39 P.3d 525 (2002)(en banc), *citing State v. Schrock*, 149 Ariz. 433, 441, 719 P.2d 1049, 1057 (1986). "A petitioner need not provide detailed evidence, but must provide specific factual allegations that, if true, would entitle him to relief." *United States v. Hearst*, 638 F.2d 1190, 1194 (9th Cir. 1980). Petitioner has set for specific factual allegations of ineffective assistance of counsel and should, at a minimum, be granted an evidentiary hearing.

IV.

CONCLUSION

¶48   Petitioner respectfully requests that this Court vacate his convictions and sentences and find that he is entitled to have his plea agreement (Exhibit A) re-offered. Alternatively, Petitioner requests that this Court permit him to file an initial petition for post-conviction relief without any preclusion effect.

RESPECTFULLY SUBMITTED this XX day of XXXXX, XXXX.

THE HOPKINS LAW OFFICE, P.C.

/s/ _____
Cedric Martin Hopkins, Esq.
Attorney for Appellant